The Law Commission

Working Paper No. 96

**Family Law
Review of Child Law:
Custody**

D1354809

**LONDON
HER MAJESTY'S STATIONERY OFFICE**

ISBN 0 11 730177 9

THE LAW COMMISSION

Working Paper No. 96

Family Law

Review of Child Law:

Custody

Table of Contents

THE LAW COMMISSION

WORKING PAPER NO. 96

REVIEW OF CHILD LAW:
CUSTODY

Summary

This consultative paper is the second in a series about the law relating to the upbringing of children.

It examines the many different statutory jurisdictions in which issues of custody and access may be determined between parents or others and identifies numerous gaps, inconsistencies and other deficiencies. A new, unified and simplified system is proposed, which is designed to reflect the responsibilities involved in bringing up a child, rather than the current proprietorial or "rights" based concepts of custody and access.

A supplement will deal with current practice in the divorce and domestic courts and a later paper will cover the wardship jurisdiction.

THE LAW COMMISSION

WORKING PAPER NO. 96

FAMILY LAW

REVIEW OF CHILD LAW

CUSTODY

PART 1

INTRODUCTION

1.1   In this paper we consider the statutory powers of the courts concerning the custody of children and make suggestions for reform.

1.2   The paper forms part of our review of the private law relating to the upbringing of children[1] and is the second in the series which began with our Working Paper on Guardianship.[2] This whole area of law is bedevilled by the complication and duplication of remedies and procedures which have developed according to no clear principle.   It is also quite unintelligible to the ordinary person, including the very families who

---

1   Nineteenth Annual Report 1983 - 1984 (1985) Law Com. No. 140, para. 2.28.

2   (1985) Working Paper No. 91.

ought to be able to know and understand their position.[3]   Hence, we hope that it will prove possible to bring together into a single comprehensive code[4] the many concepts and procedures used in private law to allocate responsibility for children amongst individuals.   Our aim is to produce a single report, with draft legislation to that end.

1.3   In the earlier paper we explained our underlying objectives thus: on a technical level, we wish to rationalise and simplify a system which contains many gaps, inconsistencies and unnecessary complexities; more importantly, however, we wish to ensure that the law itself accords as best it can with the first and paramount consideration of the welfare of the children involved.[5]   A simpler and more rational system must not be achieved at the expense of the very people whom it is, or should be, designed to serve.

---

3   "I am afraid the case shows that our statutory law about children, and most of our law on the subject is statutory, is in a sorry state of disarray and is not properly co-ordinated.   It is overfull of complication.   I do not suggest that a children's code should be capable of being understood by children, but I strongly feel that it should be capable of ready understanding as to powers and jurisdictions of courts by those who have to bring the matter of children before the courts": per Comyn J. quoted by Roskill L.J. in Re. C. (Wardship and Adoption) (1981) 2 F.L.R. 177, 184.

4   By codification we mean the collection of all the relevant principles and remedies into statutory form; as Lord Scarman observed in "Law Reform: The British Experience", The Jawaharlal Nehru Memorial Lectures (1979), "once a branch of the law has become statutory in character, codification is the logical, indeed the inevitable conclusion."

5   Working Paper No. 91, para. 1.4.

1.4   These objectives are particularly important in respect of the
custody jurisdictions, where the care and upbringing of a great many
children is decided each year.[6]   There is always concern for children
whose parents' marriages end in divorce, and this was demonstrated
recently by the terms of reference and recommendations of the
Matrimonial Causes Procedure Committee,[7] but they form only part of
the picture.   There are at least twelve separate enactments enabling
final orders for custody or access to be made:[8] in proceedings for
divorce, nullity or judicial separation, in other matrimonial proceedings
for financial relief, and in cases which are solely concerned with custody
and access, under the Guardianship of Minors Act 1971 to 1973 and under
the Children Act 1975, and also as an alternative to adoption.   These
provisions are neither clear nor consistent on such important matters as
the meaning of custody, who may apply, which children are concerned,
how their own point of view may be put before the court, what kinds of
order may be made and what test the court should apply.   The different
powers are classic examples of ad hoc legislation designed for particular
situations without full regard to how they fit into the wider picture.

---

6   The futures of at least 170,000 children were considered by the
     courts under these jurisdictions in 1984: (a) the parents of 148,600
     children under 16 divorced (OPCS Monitor FM 2 85/1, Table 7); (b)
     17,890 custody and access orders, other than interim, were made in
     guardianship and domestic proceedings by magistrates' courts (Home
     Office Statistical Bulletin 24/85, Table 2); (c) 1,898 orders were
     made under the Guardianship of Minors Act 1971 and the
     Guardianship Act 1973 in the High Court and county courts (Judicial
     Statistics Annual Report 1984 (1985) Cmnd. 9599, Table 4.4).   The
     latter figure includes orders relating to guardianship, maintenance
     and interim orders.   However each order in (b) or (c) may relate to
     more than one child.

7   Report of the Matrimonial Causes Procedure Committee (1985)
     Chairman: The Honourable Mrs. Justice Booth.

8   See para. 2.5 below.

1.5   Overlying the courts' statutory powers to make orders is the wardship jurisdiction of the High Court. This jurisdiction is not strictly concerned with the award of custody, because the effect of wardship is that custody is vested in the court itself[9] and the court cannot divest itself of custody without bringing the wardship to an end. We intend to consider wardship in a separate paper, but it is important here to remember that one of its current uses is to cover just those cases which are outside the net of the statutory powers.

1.6   In Part II of this paper we examine the courts' present powers in some detail and identify the questions which would have to be resolved before a single comprehensive code could be drafted. One obvious difficulty is that the provisions which may be best suited to the needs of children whose future falls to be decided in one context may not be so suitable in others. In Part III we set out what we believe the objectives of a good custody law to be. In Part IV we discuss the allocation of custody between parents, while in Part V we consider the position of non-parents. In Part VI we examine what is meant by the provision that, in issues of custody and upbringing, the court "shall regard the welfare of the minor as the first and paramount consideration", whether any problems arise in its application, and in particular whether sufficient weight is given to the wishes and feelings of the child himself. In Part VII we summarise the options canvassed throughout the paper and draw together those which we provisionally prefer in order to give an outline of a possible new scheme for the allocation of parental responsibilities. We also discuss whether that scheme should be embodied in a single statutory code. As the preceding discussion is long and complicated it may be helpful to look at Part VII before turning to the more detailed analysis on which it is based.

---

9   Re C.B. [1981] 1 W.L.R. 379, 387-388 per Ormrod L.J.

1.7   Throughout the paper we refer to a child as "he", a custodial parent as "she" and a non-custodial parent as "he". This is simply the most convenient way of distinguishing between them and, although in fact most custodial parents are women and most non-custodial parents are men, no particular significance is intended. Also, for convenience and to avoid undue length, we have used in the footnotes abbreviated references to certain statutes, reports and cases which are frequently cited.

1.8   The present law gives a wide discretion to the courts, including the magistrates' domestic courts, county courts and the High Court. Essential background information in considering reform of the law, therefore, includes the practice and approach of the courts in applying it. Some valuable studies of the practice of divorce courts in the 1970s have been published[10] and we have sought to supplement them with more limited information relating to the 1980s.[11] This consists partly of a study of magistrates' domestic courts in the north east of

---

10   Elston, Fuller and Murch, "Judicial Hearings of Undefended Divorce Petitions" (1975) 38 M.L.R. 609; Maidment, "A Study in Child Custody" (1976) 6 Fam. Law 195 and 236; Eekelaar and Clive with Clarke and Raikes, Custody After Divorce (1977) Family Law Studies No. 1, Centre for Socio-Legal Studies, Wolfson College, Oxford; Eekelaar, "Children in Divorce: Some Further Data" [1982] O.J.L.S. 63; Davis, MacLeod and Murch, "Undefended Divorce: Should Section 41 of the Matrimonial Causes Act 1973 be Repealed?" (1983) 46 M.L.R. 121; Dodds, "Children and Divorce" [1983] J.S.W.L. 228.

11   No information is as yet available about the custodianship provisions of the Children Act 1975 which came into force on 1 December 1985.

England, carried out by Mrs. J.A. Priest of the University of Durham, and partly of a study of divorce and county courts carried out within the Commission. We intend to publish the results shortly in a supplement to this Working Paper[12] and will refer to them in the course of this paper. We also hope that the information will be of general interest to those concerned about the welfare of children in divorce and similar cases.

---

12   Priest and Whybrow, <u>Custody Law in Practice in the Divorce and Domestic Courts</u> (1986).

PART II

THE STATUTORY PROVISIONS

2.1   The object of this part of the paper is to consider the present statutory powers of the courts in relation to custody and access, to identify the gaps, inconsistencies and anomalies within those powers, and to pose questions which ought to be resolved, either for their own sake or for the purpose of combining the present powers in a single comprehensive code. For convenience, these questions are collected at the end of each section, but it is not intended that an answer be supplied to each and every one. The discussion is necessarily long and detailed because of the state of the law which it reflects.

A.   Equality of parental rights

2.2   The courts' powers to make custody and access orders must be seen in the context of the legal position where no order is made.   Section 1(1) of the Guardianship Act 1973 provides:

> "In relation to the legal custody or upbringing of a minor, and in relation to the administration of any property belonging to or held in trust for a minor or the application of income of any such property, a mother shall have the same rights and authority as the law allows to a father, and the rights and authority of mother and father shall be equal and be exercisable by either without the other."

This provision must now be read against section 85(3) of the Children Act 1975:

> "Where two or more persons have a parental right or duty jointly, any one of them may exercise or perform it in any manner without the other or others if the other or, as the case may be, one or more of the others have not signified disapproval of its exercise or performance in that manner."

It is not wholly clear whether the equal rights and authority conferred by section 1(1) of the 1973 Act are "joint", so as to attract the provisions of section 85(3) of the 1975 Act, but the prevalent view is that they are,[1] and that section 85(3) accordingly modifies section 1(1) by prohibiting a parent from independently exercising a parental right or duty where the other has signified disapproval.

2.3   Section 1(2) of the 1973 Act provides that neither parent can surrender the rights and authority conferred by section 1(1), except by an agreement between husband and wife which is to operate only during their separation whilst married, but even this shall not be enforced if it will not be for the benefit of the child to do so.   Section 1(3) enables the mother or father to apply to the court for its direction where they disagree upon any question affecting their child's welfare.   The court may then make such order "regarding the matters in difference as it may think proper", but cannot make an order for custody or access.[2]   Section 1(3) is not limited to cases in which the parental powers and responsibilities in question are still shared.   Thus it appears that the section could be invoked where, for example, a father had been deprived of custody but disagreed with the mother's decision to authorise a surgical operation. We have no knowledge of the section ever having been used, either for this purpose or by parents who still have equal rights.   Parents who are not separating are unlikely to ask the court to resolve a disagreement, and if they are separating the appropriate orders will usually be for custody and access.   Moreover, there are no associated powers to make financial orders, which might be needed before a dispute over, say, education could be satisfactorily resolved.

---

1   See e.g. Bromley, Family Law 6th ed. (1981), pp. 281-282;   Bevan and Parry, Children Act 1975 (1979), para. 229.

2   Guardianship Act (G.A.) 1973, s. 1(4).

2.4   Illegitimate children are not covered by these provisions, but by section 85(7) of the Children Act 1975:

> "Except as otherwise provided by or under any enactment, while the mother of an illegitimate child is living she has the parental rights and duties exclusively."

The father may apply for access or custody, which will bring with it certain other rights, and in our Report on Illegitimacy we recommended a procedure for allowing him to apply for full parental rights and duties.[3]

> (Q1) Are parents' independent powers of action now qualified by the power of veto applicable to those who hold a parental right or duty jointly?

> (Q2) Should the power to resolve disputed questions between parents under section 1(3), Guardianship Act 1973, include the power to award custody, access or financial provision?

B.   The courts' powers

2.5   An outline of the various ways in which the basic position can be modified, by guardianship following the death of one or both parents, by adoption, and by the intervention of public law, was given in our

---

3   Law Com. No. 118 (1982), paras. 7.26-7.33 and Cl. 4 of the annexed Family Law Reform Bill.   Section 1(3) would apply to resolve disputes if, but only if, the father had been granted parental rights and duties other than access;   section 1(2) would apply to agreements between married or unmarried parents, but only as to the exercise of parental rights and duties during any period when they were not living together: see draft Family Law Reform Bill, Cl. 12.

Guardianship paper.[4] The most common modifications are, however, by means of custody and access orders. The twelve provisions under which the courts may make final orders for custody and access are as follows:

(a)   under section 42(1), Matrimonial Causes Act 1973, for the custody (including access)[5] and education of children of the family[6] in divorce, nullity or judicial separation proceedings;

(b)   under section 42(2), Matrimonial Causes Act 1973, with respect to the custody (including access) of children of the family where an order is made in proceedings between spouses for financial provision under section 27 of that Act;

(c)   under section 8(2), Domestic Proceedings and Magistrates' Courts Act 1978, regarding the legal custody of and access to children of the family in proceedings between spouses for financial provision under sections 1, 6 or 7 of that Act;

(d)   under section 14, Domestic Proceedings and Magistrates' Courts Act 1978, upon the application of a grandparent for access to a child where there is a custody order under section 8(2) of that Act;

---

4   Working Paper No. 91, paras. 1.12-1.27.

5   Matrimonial Causes Act (M.C.A.) 1973, s. 52(1).

6   See para. 2.13 below.

(e)   under section 9(1), Guardianship of Minors Act 1971, upon the application of the mother or father of a legitimate or illegitimate[7] child for legal custody or access;

(f)   under section 10(1), Guardianship of Minors Act 1971, dealing with legal custody and access where an order has been made under section 4(4) of that Act that a testamentary guardian shall be sole guardian to the exclusion of a surviving parent;[8]

(g)   under section 11(a), Guardianship of Minors Act 1971, dealing with legal custody and access where a dispute between joint guardians, one of whom is a surviving parent of the child, falls to be decided under section 7 of that Act;[9]

(h)   under section 14A(1), Guardianship of Minors Act 1971, upon the application of a grandparent for access to a legitimate or illegitimate[10] child where there is a custody order under section 9(1) of that Act;

---

7   Guardianship of Minors Act (G.M.A.) 1971, s. 14(1).

8   Section 10 can only be invoked where a testamentary guardian has himself applied for his appointment to be confirmed against a surviving parent who is also a guardian (s. 4(4)). Section 10 seems intended to be invoked by the guardian rather than the parent, who already has a right to apply for legal custody or access under s. 9. Moreover s. 10 cannot be invoked by the father of an illegitimate child unless he has a custody order in his favour under s. 9 (G.M.A. 1971, s. 14(3)).

9   It seems that either guardian may apply, though the guardian who is a surviving parent could also apply under s. 9.

10   G.M.A. 1971, s. 14A (9).

(i) under section 14A(2), Guardianship of Minors Act 1971, upon the application of a grandparent for access to a legitimate or illegitimate child where the parent who is the grandparent's child is dead;

(j) under section 33(1), Children Act 1975, upon the application of qualified persons[11] for legal custody (known here as custodianship) of children living with them;

(k) under section 34(1)(a), Children Act 1975, upon the application of a parent[12] or grandparent[13] for access to a legitimate or illegitimate child where there is a custodianship order under section 33(1) of that Act;

(l) under section 19, Children Act 1975, empowering the court to postpone determination of an application for adoption and vest legal custody of the child in the applicants[14] for a probationary period of not more than two years.

---

11   See para. 2.24 below.

12   Children Act (C.A.) 1975, s. 34(2) which says that references in subsection (1) to the child's mother or father include any person in relation to whom the child was treated as a child of the family (as defined in M.C.A. 1973, s. 52(1)).

13   Section 34(4).

14   C.A. 1975, ss. 10(1) and 11(1).

2.6 The provisions relating to custody give ancillary powers to make interim orders,[15] supervision orders,[16] or orders committing the child to the care of a local authority,[17] and to resolve disputed questions between people holding a parental right or duty jointly.[18] These will be mentioned later. Wherever there is power to make a custody order, there are also powers to order financial provision for the child.[19] The substance of these powers has received consideration in recent years[20] and we do not intend to reconsider them here. We contemplate, however, that some if not all of them would be included in any comprehensive code.[21]

---

15   M.C.A. 1973, s. 42; Domestic Proceedings and Magistrates' Courts Act (D.P.M.C.A.) 1978, s. 19; G.A. 1973, s. 2(4)(b); C.A. 1975, s. 34(5), which applies the provisions of G.A. 1973, s. 2(4).

16   M.C.A. 1973, s. 44(1); D.P.M.C.A. 1978, s. 9; G.A. 1973, s. 2(2)(a); C.A. 1975, s. 34(5). There are no corresponding provisions relating to custody orders under s. 10 or s. 11 of the G.M.A. 1971 (parent-guardian disputes).

17   M.C.A. 1973, s. 43; D.P.M.C.A. 1978, s. 10, G.A. 1973, ss. 2(2)(b) and 4; C.A. 1975, s. 34(5). There are no corresponding provisions relating to applications for custody orders under s. 10 or s. 11 of the G.M.A. 1971 (parent-guardian disputes).

18   D.P.M.C.A. 1978, s. 13; C.A. 1975, s. 38.

19   G.M.A. 1971, s. 9(2); D.P.M.C.A. 1978, ss. 2, 6, 7 and 11(1); M.C.A. 1973, s. 23(2); C.A. 1975, s. 34.

20   See Financial Provision in Matrimonial Proceedings (1969) Law Com. No. 25, Matrimonial Proceedings in Magistrates' Courts (1976) Law Com. No. 77, Financial Consequences of Divorce: The Basic Policy. A Discussion Paper (1980) Law Com. No. 103, and The Response to the Law Commission's Discussion Paper, and Recommendations on the Policy of the Law (1981) Law Com. No. 112.

21   See paras. 2.12 and 7.46 and 7.47 below.

2.7   In addition to the provisions listed above, the Review of Child Care Law has recommended that a court hearing care proceedings or discharging a care order should have power to make a custody order and to deal with questions of access and supervision relating to it at the same time.[22]

C.   When the courts' powers arise

2.8   It will be apparent from the above list that the courts' powers to deal with custody and access arise in two different ways:

(a)   upon the application for that purpose of a person regarded as qualified to begin proceedings relating to that particular child;[23] or

(b)   in the course of proceedings for other relief, usually between spouses.[24]

The power to make orders in matrimonial proceedings raises several questions which would have to be resolved before a single code could be devised.

2.9   First, there is power to deal with custody of children who are concerned in divorce, nullity or judicial separation proceedings between

---

22   Such orders could only be made in favour of parents or spouses who had treated the child as a child of the family or persons who would qualify to apply for a custodianship order or where the grounds for a care order exist.   Review of Child Care Law ("R.C.C.L.") (1985), paras. 19.7, 19.9, 19.11 and 20.27.

23   G.M.A. 1971, ss. 9(1) and 14A(2); C.A. 1975, s. 33(1).

24   M.C.A. 1973, ss. 42(1) and 42(2); D.P.M.C.A. 1978, s. 8(2); G.M.A. 1971, ss. 10(1), 11(a); C.A. 1975, s. 19.

spouses[25] or in proceedings for financial relief between spouses,[26] but these do not exhaust the range of statutory matrimonial remedies in which the welfare of children may be an important factor. In particular, there is no power to deal with custody or access in the course of proceedings for personal protection under section 16 of the Domestic Proceedings and Magistrates' Courts Act 1978, or for an injunction under section 1 of the Domestic Violence and Matrimonial Proceedings Act 1976, or for an order affecting rights of occupation in the matrimonial home under section 1 of the Matrimonial Homes Act 1983. Yet the question of custody or interim custody of any children involved is often of great importance in resolving the issue between the parties.[27] Usually, this can be dealt with by simultaneous proceedings under section 9(1) of the Guardianship of Minors Act. However, these require an application by the mother or father of the child, whereas the spouses may not be or both be parents of the child. Even between parents, the 1971 Act may not match the courts' powers under the other enactments (for example, as to the grounds for, and duration of, interim orders).[28] Insofar as this may encourage spouses to begin divorce proceedings prematurely it may be undesirable.

2.10   Secondly, in some matrimonial proceedings the court has a positive duty to consider the future of certain children, even if the adults are in agreement about it. In divorce, nullity and judicial separation

---

25   M.C.A. 1973, s. 42(1).

26   M.C.A. 1973, s. 42(2); D.P.M.C.A. 1978, s. 8(2).

27   For example, when making an order under s. 1 of the Matrimonial Homes Act 1983, the court must have regard to the needs of any children and all the circumstances of the case (s. 1(3)); see also e.g. Essex County Council v. T., T. v. T., The Times, 15 March 1986.

28   See paras. 2.70 and 2.71 below.

proceedings, the court is required to consider what is proposed for the children's welfare and in general final relief cannot be granted unless proper arrangements are made.[29]   In proceedings for financial relief under the Domestic Proceedings and Magistrates' Courts Act 1978, the court must not dismiss or make a final order on the application until it has decided whether to exercise its powers to deal with custody and access and, if so, in what way.[30]   There is no equivalent requirement in proceedings for financial relief under section 27 of the Matrimonial Causes Act 1973.

2.11   Thirdly, the court may deal with custody and access under the 1978 Act whether or not it makes an order for financial provision.[31]   It may also deal with such matters where divorce, nullity or judicial separation proceedings are dismissed, either forthwith or within a reasonable period after the dismissal, but only if dismissal happens after the beginning of the trial.[32]   In proceedings for financial relief under section 27 of the 1973 Act, on the other hand, the court may only deal with custody (including access) where financial provision is ordered; furthermore, any order will only have effect while an order for financial provision is in force.[33]

2.12   Finally, where the court has power to deal with custody and access irrespective of the outcome of the proceedings between the adults,

---

29   M.C.A. 1973, s. 41(1); this procedure is discussed in paras. 4.4-4.16 below.

30   D.P.M.C.A. 1978, s. 8(1).

31   D.P.M.C.A. 1978, s. 8(2).

32   In 1984 there were 975 divorces entered for trial out of a total of 178,940 petitions: Judicial Statistics Annual Report 1984 (1985) Cmnd. 9599, Table 4.5.

33   M.C.A. 1973, s. 42(2).

it also has power to award financial provision for the child.[34]   Were all
these powers to be covered by a single statute, it would be desirable for
that statute also to deal with financial provision and property adjustment
for children.   This would entail separating the provisions relating to
children involved in divorce and similar proceedings from those relating to
the adults.   This may be undesirable, as provision for the children and the
adults are inextricably linked[35] and in relation to both the courts are now
required to give first consideration to the children's welfare.[36]

> (Q3) Should the courts retain power to award custody and
> access, of their own motion, in the course of other
> proceedings?

> (Q4) If so, should the proceedings concerned be extended to
> include, for example, applications for personal protection, for
> injunctions, or for orders under the Matrimonial Homes Act
> 1983?

> (Q5) Should the courts' duty to consider the arrangements
> made or proposed for all the children involved be the same in
> all such proceedings?

> (Q6) Should the power to award custody or access in such
> proceedings arise irrespective of the outcome of the case
> between the adult parties?

---

34   M.C.A. 1973, s. 23(2); D.P.M.C.A. 1978, s. 11(1).

35   Law Com. No. 112 (op. cit. at n. 20), para. 24.   See, e.g., Milliken-
Smith v. Milliken-Smith [1970] 1 W.L.R. 793, Robinson v. Robinson
(1973) 2 F.L.R. 1, 16 per Scarman L.J., Ackerman v. Ackerman
[1972] Fam. 225, 233 per Phillimore L.J., Calderbank v. Calderbank
[1976] Fam. 93, 102 per Scarman L.J.

36   M.C.A. 1973, s. 25(1); D.P.M.C.A. 1978, s. 3(1).

D. The adults and children involved

In matrimonial cases

2.13   The matrimonial proceedings in which orders for custody and access may be made will, of course, be initiated between husband and wife.[37] The courts' powers, however, are not limited to the children of their marriage or even to the children of one or both parties. Under both the Matrimonial Causes Act 1973 and the Domestic Proceedings and Magistrates' Courts Act 1978, the court may make orders relating to any "child of the family" who is under the age of eighteen. In the former:[38]

> "'child of the family', in relation to the parties to a marriage, means -
>
> (a)   a child of both of those parties; and
>
> (b)   any other child, not being a child who has been boarded out with those parties by a local authority or voluntary organisation, who has been treated by both of those parties as a child of their family;"

Adopted, legitimated[39] or illegitimate[40] children are included under (a)

---

37   Matrimonial Causes Rules 1977, r. 13 provides that other persons shall become parties, e.g. where the respondent has committed adultery, the person with whom the adultery is alleged to have been committed will usually be made a co-respondent, r. 13(1).

38   M.C.A. 1973, s. 52(1); c.f. D.P.M.C.A. 1978, s. 88(1).

39   Legitimacy Act 1976, s. 2.

40   M.C.A. 1973, s. 52(1) states that "child, in relation to one or both of the parties to a marriage, includes an illegitimate child of that party or, as the case may be, of both parties". There will be a few cases where an illegitimate child of both parties is not legitimated by their marriage e.g. where, at the date of the marriage, the father is domiciled in a foreign country whose laws do not legitimate children on such marriages.

or (b) as the facts dictate. The sole difference between this definition and that in the 1978 Act is that the latter only excludes a child who currently "is being" boarded-out by a local authority or voluntary organisation.

2.14   Whether a child has been treated as a member of the spouses' family is a question of fact.   Both spouses must have treated him as such;[41] some behaviour towards the child is required, so behaviour before the child is born does not suffice;[42] there must also be a "family" in which to include the child, so that behaviour after the spouses have separated again will not suffice;[43] if the spouses have included the child in their family, however, the fact that the husband did so in the mistaken belief that the child was his own will not affect the matter.[44]   The rationale behind this wide provision is that, if a child has been treated as part of the spouses' common household, it is as much his home as anyone else's which is breaking up.[45]   It is therefore thought right that the court should oversee, and if necessary determine, the arrangements made for his future.   That rationale does not exist where a local authority or voluntary organisation is responsible for the child's welfare under the Boarding-out of Children Regulations.[46]   The 1978 Act may be preferable to the 1973 Act in expressly excluding only those who are currently

---

41   See A. v. A. (Family: Unborn Child) [1974] Fam. 6.

42   Ibid.

43   M. v. M. (Child of the Family) (1980) 2 F.L.R. 39.

44   A. v. A. (Family: Unborn Child) [1974] Fam. 6.   See also Law Com. No. 25 (op. cit. at n. 20), paras. 25 - 29.

45   See further paras. 5.6-5.11 below.

46   Child Care Act 1980, ss. 21(1)(a) and 61; S.I. 1955 No. 1217.

19

boarded-out but not those who are no longer in care, for example because a custodianship order has been made.[47]

2.15   However, the present definition also covers children who no longer have any home with the spouses.   Once a child has been treated as a child of the family the jurisdiction exists whether or not the treatment continues.   On the other hand, while a non-parent spouse may thus be granted custody or access in the course of matrimonial proceedings he cannot initiate such proceedings solely for this purpose.

2.16   The 1973 and 1978 Acts are also not consistent as to the effect of any custody or access order upon the legal position of any parent who is not a party to the marriage.   Under the 1973 Act, an order does not affect the rights of any person who is not a party to the marriage "unless the child is the child of one or both parties to the marriage and that person was a party to the proceedings for an order."[48]   Hence proceedings between a parent and step-parent will bind the other parent only if that other parent is a party to them; proceedings between non-parents, such as informal foster parents or even a guardian and his wife, cannot affect the rights of any other person even if that person is made a party.

2.17   There is no equivalent provision in the 1978 Act.   However, the court cannot exercise its powers under that Act in respect of a child who is not a child of both parties to the marriage unless any parent is present or represented or adequate steps have been taken to give the

---

47   "Has been boarded out" could, however, mean "has been and is boarded out".   The exclusion does not cover all children in care, e.g. those currently "home on trial" with a parent, guardian, relative or friend under Child Care Act 1980, s. 21(2).

48   M.C.A. 1973, s. 42(5).

parent an opportunity of attending the hearing.[49]   Any parent who is present or represented at the hearing must be given an opportunity of making representations to the court.[50]   It appears, therefore, that if these steps are taken, the order will bind.

2.18   Once matrimonial proceedings are brought where there is a child of the family under eighteen, the court may make custody and access orders in favour of people who are neither parents nor parties to the marriage in question.   Here again, the 1973 and 1978 Acts are not consistent.   In the 1973 Act, the court's powers are expressed as if exercisable of its own motion and there is no restriction upon exercising them in favour of third parties.   In practice, however, third parties may be given leave to intervene in the suit in order to seek custody or access[51] and under the rules certain people may intervene without leave.

---

49   D.P.M.C.A. 1978, s. 12(2);   see also Magistrates' Courts (Matrimonial Proceedings) Rules 1980, r. 9;   but not the father of any illegitimate child unless he has been judicially found to be such.

50   D.P.M.C.A. 1978, s. 12(1).

51   Chetwynd v. Chetwynd [1865] 4 Sw. & Tr. 151: "It was the obvious intention of the legislature that the court should have the power to make such orders as it might think necessary for the benefit of the children themselves;   and it could not properly exercise that most useful power if it were to decline altogether to hear what a third person had to say on the matter .... [w]hen any third person shows sufficient cause to justify his intervention, he ought to be allowed to intervene";   per the Judge Ordinary.   The right of third parties to apply for leave to intervene was clearly recognised in the Matrimonial Causes Rules 1950, r. 54(1) (revoked) but is less explicit in the current Matrimonial Causes Rules 1977, r. 92(3): "without prejudice to the right of any other person entitled to apply for an order as respects a child".   For recent cases in which custody was awarded to third parties intervening, see Morgan v. Morgan (1974) 4 Fam. Law 189 (aunt and uncle) and Cahill v. Cahill (1974) 5 Fam. Law 16 (grandparents).

These are (a) a guardian[52] or step-parent, or (b) a person who has custody or control of the child under a court order, or (c) a local authority having care or supervision of the child by an order under the Matrimonial Causes Act itself.[53] Once there has been a divorce, third parties may intervene at any time; the most obvious example is a step-parent who has married one of the divorced parents and wishes now to have custody or joint custody with that parent.[54] It might be thought that no such order could be made after the divorce suit has abated upon the death of one of the parties to the marriage. Nevertheless, there have been cases where custody has been awarded to a third party after the death of the custodial parent.[55]

2.19   Under the 1978 Act, the court's powers are also expressed as exercisable of its own motion, but limits are laid down. Legal custody or access can be granted to either of the parties to the marriage or to any other person who is a parent of the child.[56] It is not clear whether "parent" for this purpose includes the father of an illegitimate child. The normal rule of construction is that the word "parent" in an Act of

---

52   This includes testamentary guardians, appointed under G.M.A. 1971 ss. 3 and 4 and guardians appointed by the court under G.M.A. 1971 ss. 3, 5 and 6. It may also include parents as they are not mentioned elsewhere. If step-parents do not need leave to intervene it is probable that parents are similarly excused.

53   Matrimonial Causes Rules 1977, r. 92(3).

54   See paras. 2.26 and 2.32 below.

55   Pryor v. Pryor [1947] P. 64, where the parents of a deceased mother, whose marriage had been dissolved, were given leave to intervene in her divorce suit and were awarded custody of the children of the marriage.

56   D.P.M.C.A. 1978, ss. 8(2) and (3).

Parliament does not include him unless the context otherwise requires.[57] Illegitimate children are only expressly included in these provisions in relation to the parties to the marriage.[58] The father can, of course, apply for custody or access under the Guardianship of Minors Act 1971, so that the point is one of procedure rather than substance.[59]

2.20   As to the other third parties, where the court makes an order for legal custody, a grandparent of the child (including an illegitimate child)[60] may apply for the court "to make such order requiring access to the child to be given to the grandparent as the court thinks fit".[61] There is no power to grant access to any other third party. Where the court is of the opinion that legal custody should be given to someone other than a party to the marriage or a parent, it may direct that person to be treated as if he had applied for legal custody (known as custodianship) under the Children Act 1975.[62] The person is then regarded as qualified to apply

---

57   Re M. (An Infant) [1955] 2 Q.B. 479; c.f. draft Family Law Reform Bill annexed to Law Com. No. 118 (op. cit. at n. 3), cls. 5, 6, 7, 9, 10 and 12, in which "parent" is meant to include the father of a non-marital child.

58   D.P.M.C.A. 1978, s. 88(1); M.C.A. 1973, s. 52(1); see n. 40 above.

59   Section 9(1); see para. 2.21 below.

60   D.P.M.C.A. 1978, s. 14(6). It is not clear whether the parent must be legitimate, but there seems no obvious reason for displacing the ordinary rule of construction that the term only includes legitimate relationships.

61   D.P.M.C.A. 1978, s. 14(1).

62   D.P.M.C.A. 1978, s. 8(3); see para. 2.24 below.

under that Act even if he would not otherwise have been so. Most of the provisions of the 1975 Act relating to custodianship are then attracted.[63]

(Q7) Spouses may seek custody and access in respect of children of the family who are not their own, but only in the course of a claim for matrimonial relief (or, in the case of access, where there is a custodianship order): should they be able to apply independently?

(Q8) The definitions of "child of the family" in the Matrimonial Causes Act 1973 and Domestic Proceedings and Magistrates' Courts Act 1978 are not identical: which, if either, is preferable? Are there other respects in which the definition requires amendment?

(Q9) The effect of an order under each Act upon a parent who is not a party to the marriage in question is not identical: which, if either, is preferable?

(Q10) Under the 1973 Act, the courts have unrestricted power to grant custody to third parties, whereas under the 1978 Act, custody may only be granted to either spouse, a parent (which may not include the father of an illegitimate child), or to a third party by means of custodianship: which is preferable?

(Q11) Under the 1973 Act, the courts have unrestricted power to grant access to third parties, whereas under the 1978 Act, access may only be granted to either spouse or to a parent, or

---

63   The requirements for the child's residence with the third party and the consent of a person with legal custody (C.A. 1975, s. 33(3)) are dispensed with and C.A. 1975, s. 37(4) disapplies the provision (C.A. 1975, s. 40) which requires notice of an application for custodianship to be given to the local authority.

(provided that there is a custody order) to a grandparent: should the categories of those who may be awarded access under the latter Act be extended?

In Guardianship of Minors Act cases

2.21   Under section 9 of the Guardianship of Minors Act 1971, either the mother or father of a legitimate or illegitimate child may apply for the court to "make such order regarding (a) the legal custody of the minor and (b) the right of access to the minor of his mother or father, as the court thinks fit ...". There is no general provision for third parties to apply, but once again if a legal custody order is made under the section, a grandparent may apply for such access as the court thinks fit,[64] and if the court is of the opinion that legal custody should be granted to someone other than the mother or father it may direct that person to be treated as if he had applied for custodianship,[65] with the same effects as an equivalent direction under the 1978 Act.[66]

2.22   The court has powers, expressed as of its own motion, to make legal custody and access orders, under section 10(1) of the 1971 Act, where it has ordered a person to be sole guardian to the exclusion of a surviving parent,[67] and under section 11(a), where there is a disagreement between joint guardians, one of whom is a surviving parent, on any matter affecting the welfare of the child.[68] There is no apparent restriction on

---

64   G.M.A. 1971, s. 14A(1).   Section 14A(9) provides that the child may be illegitimate.   As to the legitimacy of the parents, see n. 60 above.

65   C.A. 1975, s. 37(3).

66   See para. 2.20 and n. 63 above.

67   See n. 8 above.

68   G.M.A. 1971, s. 7; see n. 9 above.

the court's power to award custody to a third party under either of these sections and the custodianship provisions are not attracted. Access, on the other hand, can only be awarded to the surviving parent.

2.23   However, under section 14A(2) of the 1971 Act, where one parent of a legitimate or illegitimate child is dead,[69] or both parents are dead, a grandparent who is a parent of the child's deceased parent may apply for such access as the court thinks fit. The parent of a surviving parent of the child cannot apply. It is not clear whether "deceased parent" for this purpose includes the father of an illegitimate child[70] or whether the parents of a deceased parent who is illegitimate could apply.[71]

> (Q12) Under the Guardianship of Minors Act 1971, courts have unrestricted power to award custody to third parties in disputes between surviving parents and guardians, but otherwise must do so by means of custodianship: which is preferable?

> (Q13) Under the 1971 Act, courts may award access to either parent, or (provided that there is a custody order) to a grandparent: should the categories be extended?

> (Q14) Under the 1971 Act, a grandparent who is the parent of the child's deceased parent may apply for access: should the circumstances or categories be extended?

---

69   G.M.A. 1971, s. 14A(9).

70   See para. 2.19 above.

71   See n. 60 above.

2.24   Where there are no matrimonial or Guardianship of Minors Act proceedings on foot, the only statutory powers to make orders for legal custody and access are the custodianship provisions of the Children Act 1975.[72] The following are qualified to apply:[73]

> "(a) a relative or step-parent of the child -
>
>> (i)   who applies with the consent of a person having legal custody of the child, and
>>
>> (ii)   with whom the child has had his home for the three months preceding the making of the application;
>
> (b)   any person -
>
>> (i)   who applies with the consent of a person having legal custody of the child, and
>>
>> (ii)   with whom the child has had his home for a period or periods before the making of the application which amount to at least twelve months and include the three months preceding the making of the application;
>
> (c)   any person with whom the child had his home for a period or periods before the making of the application which amount to at least three years and include the three months preceding the making of the application."

2.25   The "mother or father" of the child is not qualified under any of these three heads.[74] Although the word "parent" does not usually

---

72   Part II, ss. 33-46, which came into force on 1 December 1985.   See also D.H.S.S. Circular LAC (85)13.

73   C.A. 1975, s. 33(3).

74   C.A. 1975, s. 33(4).

include the father of an illegitimate child, the general view is that he is covered by the term "father".[75] Both he and the mother can, of course, apply under section 9 of the 1971 Act without the other qualifications as to residence and consent.

2.26   A step-parent is not qualified under any of the three heads if the child has been named in an order relating to the arrangements for his welfare in proceedings for divorce or nullity.[76] In such cases, of course, there is no need for the step-parent to seek custodianship, for an application can be made in the divorce suit.[77] However, that is true whether or not the child has been named in such an order and applies to other people as well as to step-parents, although most others must first obtain leave. The rationale of the exclusion must therefore be to ensure that, in the particular case of step-parents of children where the court has assumed responsibility for the arrangements following divorce, a later application for custody is made in the divorce suit and not elsewhere. Hence the exclusion no longer applies if the order was to the effect that there were or might be children to whom the provision applied, but about whom no declaration as to the arrangements could yet be made, and it has since been determined that the child was not a child of the family of that marriage after all.[78] Nor does the exclusion apply if "the parent other than the one the step-parent married is dead or cannot be found";[79] in these cases, it would still be open to the step-parent to apply in the

---

75   Bevan and Parry, The Children Act 1975 (1979), para. 263; Bromley, Family Law 6th ed. (1981), p. 384; Cretney, Principles of Family Law 4th ed. (1984), p. 411.

76   C.A. 1975, s. 33(5); see M.C.A. 1973, s. 41, para. 4.4 below.

77   See para. 2.18 above.

78   C.A. 1975, s. 33(8)(b); see M.C.A. 1973, s. 41(1)(c).

79   C.A. 1975, s. 33(8)(a).

divorce suit,[80] but there is less reason to require him to do so. It is still not clear why step-parents alone should be obliged to return to the divorce court, although in most cases they might prefer to do so because the procedure is less onerous.[81]

2.27   The term "step-parent" is not defined. It seems clear that it was intended to include the husband of the mother, and the wife of the father, of an illegitimate child.[82]   "Relative" is defined, to mean a grandparent, brother, sister, uncle or aunt, whether of the full or half blood or by affinity, and whether the child is legitimate or illegitimate.[83] It would therefore be surprising if parents by affinity of an illegitimate child were not included.

2.28   Only the consent of "a" person having legal custody is required for the shorter qualifying periods to apply, whereas the agreement of each parent or guardian must be given or dispensed with before an adoption

---

80   It is difficult to see the logic of this exception where the step-parent's spouse is on a third marriage. In such a case the death of the child's other parent might have no bearing on the arrangements for the child following the second divorce. The exception would also create problems if "parent" includes the parent of an illegitimate child, for the death of such a parent might have no bearing on the arrangements made following the divorce of the other parent.

81   E.g. there is no requirement of investigation by the local authority.

82   See Report of the Departmental Committee on the Adoption of Children (1972) Cmnd. 5107, Chairman (until November 1971): Sir William Houghton (the "Houghton Committee"), Ch. 5, para. 103; Bevan and Parry, The Children Act 1975 (1979), para. 277.

83   The definition is borrowed from the Adoption Act 1958, s. 57(1); C.A. 1975 s. 107(1). Although that definition also includes the father of an illegitimate child, he may be excluded by C.A. 1975, s. 33(4). See n. 75 above.

order can be made.[84]   It is clear that parents have legal custody, unless and until deprived of it, but so also does a local authority having parental powers and duties under a care order[85] or having passed a resolution assuming parental rights and duties.[86]   The consent required is to the custodianship application, rather than to the order, but there is no provision for dispensing with it.   However, if no-one has legal custody, or if the person with legal custody cannot be found, or if the applicant himself has it, then the shorter periods apply without the need for consent.[87]

2.29   The 1975 Act is explicit as to the effect of a custodianship order upon the rights of other people.   While it is in force, the right of any person (other than a parent who is the custodian's spouse) to legal custody of the child is suspended but, subject to any further order by any court, revives when the custodianship order is revoked.[88]   Thus a custodianship order does not supersede an earlier custody or care order. Where the custodian is married to a parent who already has legal custody, however, they have it jointly.[89]   The numerous defendants to an

---

84   Or the child freed for adoption, C.A. 1975, s. 12(1)(b) [Adoption Act 1976, s. 16(1)(b)].

85   Children and Young Persons Act 1969, ss. 1 and 7(7)(a); Child Care Act 1980, s. 10(2).

86   Child Care Act 1980, s. 3(1).

87   C.A. 1975, s. 33(6).

88   C.A. 1975, s. 44(1).

89   C.A. 1975, s. 44(2).

application for custodianship include not only the mother and father or guardian of the child but also any other person who has actual or legal custody of him.[90]

2.30   Where there is a custodianship order, the mother, father or grandparent of the child may apply for an order requiring such access to the child to be given as the court thinks fit.[91] For this purpose, "mother" and "father" include any person in relation to whom the child was treated as a child of the family as defined by the Matrimonial Causes Act 1973[92] and "grandparent" includes the grandparent of an illegitimate child.[93] It was clearly intended that "mother" and "father" should cover both legitimate and illegitimate relationships.

> (Q15) Do the terms "parent", and "grandparent" and "step-parent" throughout the legislation require clarification with regard to non-marital relationships?

> (Q16) Although third parties may be awarded custody or access in the course of proceedings initiated by others, only mothers and fathers, guardians, people who are qualified (by length of care and in some cases parental consent) to apply forcustodianship, and (to a very limited extent) grandparents are permitted to initiate proceedings solely relating to the

---

90   R.S.C. 0.90 r. 16(1);   C.C.R. 0.47, r. 7(3) Magistrates' Courts (Custodianship Orders) Rules 1985, r. 5(1).

91   C.A. 1975, s. 34(1)(a).

92   C.A. 1975, s. 34(2).

93   C.A. 1975, s. 34(4).   As to whether the parent must be legitimate, see n. 60 above.

custody or upbringing of a child: should the categories of people qualified to initiate be amended or extended?

(Q17) In what circumstances should people who would otherwise be qualified to apply for custodianship be obliged to seek custody in divorce or other proceedings?

(Q18) Should the consent of each person entitled to legal custody be required for the shorter periods of qualification for custodianship to apply?

(Q19) Should there be a procedure for dispensing with consent to custodianship applications?

(Q20) Is there a case for extending the categories of people who may be awarded access where a custodianship order is made?

In adoption cases

2.31   Finally, there are several provisions which enable or encourage the making of custody orders as an alternative to adoption.   Some of these have the effect of widening the range of people who may be awarded legal custody.[94]   Thus, provided that the required parental agreements have been given or dispensed with,[95] and certain other requirements[96] fulfilled, the court may postpone determination of the

---

94   For example, a foster-parent who has not had the child in his care long enough to apply for custodianship under C.A. 1975, s. 33(3)(b) may qualify to apply for an adoption order.

95   C.A. 1975, s. 12(1).

96   I.e. that in the case of a child who was not placed with the applicants by an adoption agency, three months' notice of the intention to apply for an adoption order was given to the local authority (C.A. 1975, s. 18(1)).

adoption application and grant legal custody to the applicants for a probationary period of up to two years.[97]

2.32   More importantly, once again provided that the required parental agreements have been given or dispensed with,[98] there are provisions for the court to direct that an adoption application be treated as an application for custodianship, with the same effects as the analagous directions in proceedings under the 1971 and 1978 Acts.[99] Where the adoption application is made by a relative[100] or by a step-parent who is not disqualified from applying for custodianship,[101] whether alone or jointly with his or her spouse, the court must convert the application into one for custodianship if it is satisfied (a) that the child's welfare would not be better safeguarded and promoted by the adoption order than it would be by a custodianship order, and (b) that the

---

97   C.A. 1975, s. 19.   Although the main purpose of an interim order is to test the suitability of the prospective adopters (Houghton Committee Report (op. cit. at n. 82), paras. 309 and 310) it may also be used to see whether the child's interests would best be served by some other course, e.g.   a transfer to the custody of a natural parent: S. v. Huddersfield B.C. [1975] Fam. 113.   However, in Re O. [1985] F.L.R. 546, the Divisional Court, in allowing an appeal against an interim order, said that the question the court had to answer was whether an adoption order was appropriate.   An interim order merely postponed the decision and served no useful purpose.

98   C.A. 1975, s. 12(1).

99   See paras. 2.20 and 2.21 above.

100   For the meaning of relative see para. 2.27.   The father of an illegitimate child is apparently included here, because C.A. 1975, s. 107(1) adopts the meaning in the Adoption Act 1958, s. 57(1), even though he may not be able to apply for custodianship.   See para. 2.25 above.

101   See para. 2.26 and C.A. 1975, s. 37(5).

custodianship order would be appropriate.[102]   Given the power to dispense with parental agreement to adoption,[103] it is possible that some relatives or step-parents might qualify for custodianship under these provisions when they would not do so directly. The main object, however, is to direct the mind of the court towards a less drastic solution than adoption when this is sought by relatives or by people who have become step-parents following the child's illegitimacy or the death of one of his parents.[104]   Where there have been divorce or other proceedings under the Matrimonial Causes Act 1973, and a step-parent (who will usually be disqualified from applying for custodianship) applies to adopt, whether alone or jointly with the parent to whom he or she is married, the court "shall dismiss the application if it considers that the matter would be better dealt with under section 42 (orders for custody etc.)" of the 1973 Act.[105]   It is questionable whether the disincentive in the first of these provisions, which applies where the court is satisfied that adoption would not be better, is greater or lesser than the disincentive in the second, which applies where the court is satisfied that custody would be better.[106] Where an applicant for adoption, or either applicant in a joint application, is not a relative or step-parent, the court may convert the application into one for custodianship, once again provided that the required agreements have been given or dispensed with, if it is of the opinion that a custodianship order would be more appropriate.[107]   This again can have the effect of widening the categories of those who may be awarded legal custody.

---

102   C.A. 1975, s. 37(1).

103   C.A. 1975, s. 12(1)(b)(ii) and s. 12(2).

104   Houghton Committee Report (op. cit. at n. 82), Ch. 5, paras. 120 and 121.

105   C.A. 1975, ss. 10(3) and 11(4).

106   See Re S. [1977] 3 All E.R. 671; Re D. (1980) 10 Fam. Law 246; Rawlings, "Law Reform with Tears" (1982) 45 M.L.R. 637.

107   C.A. 1975, s. 37(2).

(Q21) Should the provisions requiring courts to consider
custody or custodianship as an alternative to an adoption
application be made consistent?   If so, which approach is
preferable?

(Q22) Should it be possible to qualify for custodianship by
making an adoption application?

2.33   In summary, the effect of the provisions discussed in this
section of the paper is that, while parents are the best placed to apply to
the courts for custody and access orders relating to their children, spouses
are almost as well placed in relation to "children of the family".   Further,
once proceedings have been started between spouses or parents, other
people may be granted custody or, to a lesser extent, access.   Otherwise,
the rights of relatives, step-parents and others to apply to the courts are
strictly limited.

E.   The scope and effect of custody orders

Custody

2.34   "Custody" has its origin in the common law.   It may denote a
state of fact: in this sense a child is in the "custody" of an adult if he
happens to be under the adult's physical control.   It may also denote a
state of law, in the narrow sense of the legal power of physical control or
in the wider sense of a "bundle of powers", including not only the power of
physical control but also powers relating to a child's education, religion,
property and the general management of his life, almost the equivalent of
guardianship.[108]

2.35   Under section 42(1) of the Matrimonial Causes Act 1973, the
court has power in divorce, nullity and judicial separation proceedings to

---

108   Hewer v. Bryant [1970] 1 Q.B. 357, 368 - 370 per Lord Denning M.R.,
      372-373 per Sachs L.J.

make orders for "custody" (which is later defined to include access)[109] and "education", whereas under section 42(2) of that Act, in proceedings for financial provision, it has power only to make orders for "custody" (again including access). It might be thought from this that custody was intended in the narrower of the two senses mentioned above. However, whatever may have been meant in the first Matrimonial Causes Act of 1857, it is clear that in the twentieth century the wider meaning has been adopted and the court has been able to allocate the whole "bundle of powers" as it thinks fit.[110] The court would no doubt be loath to regard its powers under the statute as artificially restricted, particularly as divorce jurisdiction was until the Matrimonial Causes Act 1967 vested solely in the High Court, which has wide inherent powers in relation to children. Further, until the Guardianship Act 1973 gave her equal rights and authority, the mother of a legitimate child could only acquire rights by express statutory provision, court order, or on the death of the father.[111] There could well be divorce cases in which it was appropriate to make her responsible for every aspect of the child's life. On the other hand, in the days when divorces were granted for matrimonial fault, the court might be reluctant to deprive an "unimpeachable" parent of virtually the whole "bundle of powers", but might be forced to recognise that the children's interests required that they live with the other, usually the mother.[112] In such circumstances, an order giving "custody" to the

---

109   M.C.A. 1973 s. 52(1).

110   Willis v. Willis [1928] P. 10; Wakeham v. Wakeham [1954] 1 W.L.R. 366; Jane v. Jane (1983) 4 F.L.R. 712.

111   Under the Guardianship of Infants Act 1925, s. 2, the mother could apply to the court for an order concerning any matter affecting her child.

112   Wakeham v. Wakeham [1954] 1 W.L.R. 366, 369 per Denning L.J.; Allen v. Allen [1948] 2 All E.R. 413; Willoughby v. Willoughby [1951] P. 184, Singleton L.J. at p. 192: "I have yet to learn that the fact that a woman commits adultery prevents her in all circumstances from being a good mother".

father was thought to leave him in charge of the major decisions relating to the child, while giving responsibility for day-to-day matters to the mother granted "care and control".

2.36   Doubts have, however, been created by recent decisions culminating in the observations of the Court of Appeal in Dipper v. Dipper.[113] In that case, just such a "split order" had been made at first instance, giving sole custody to the father but care and control to the mother, because the judge wished the father to be notified before the children were removed from their schools and to have a say in their future upbringing.   On appeal, it was said that "to suggest that a parent with custody dominates the situation so far as education or any other serious matter is concerned is quite wrong".[114]   Not only would any disagreement between custodial and non-custodial parent have to be resolved by the court, but "the parent is always entitled, whatever his custodial status, to know and be consulted about the future education of the children and any other major matters."[115]   The court was probably here referring to the effect of an order granting sole custody including care and control to the mother, although their remarks would be equally applicable to the order in fact made in favour of the father.

2.37   These observations might appear to confine the meaning of custody to the narrow sense mentioned earlier.   It seems unlikely, however, that this was intended, for it would take away the power of the

---

113   [1981] Fam. 31.   See also B. v. B. (1978) 1 F.L.R.   87, where although the mother had custody of the child, the father was not deprived of his right to have a say in where she should be educated.

114   Ormrod L.J. at p. 45.

115   Cumming Bruce L.J. at p. 48.

court to distinguish between the wider and narrower aspects of parental powers and respsonsibilities through making an order for joint custody with care and control to one party. Such an order was agreed by the parties on appeal in the Dipper case and approved by the court. However, if a sole custody order is restricted as the court suggested,[116] it is difficult to know what difference there is between a sole custody order, a joint custody order with care and control to one party, and an order leaving parental status intact save for care and control to one party.

2.38   Technically it could be that under a sole custody order the non-custodial parent must refer disputed questions to the court, under section 1(3) of the Guardianship Act 1973 (or, subject to the meaning of "custody", under section 42(1) itself); that under a joint custody order, each parent has a power of veto over the other's decisions (save where one is excluded from matters of care and control); while under a care and control order each parent retains an independent power of action (under section 1(1) of the Guardianship Act 1973) over matters other than care and control. The reference in Dipper v. Dipper to a duty to consult is in any event difficult to understand.

2.39   Hence, both the extent of the courts' powers under the 1973 Act and the effect of custody orders, particularly upon the position of the non-custodial parent, is now unclear. In practice, it seems that some courts make sole custody orders and others make joint custody orders with

---

116   And c.f. Jane v. Jane (1983) 4 F.L.R. 712, an exceptional case where a split order giving sole custody to the father with care and control to the mother was upheld expressly so as to give the father sole control over medical treatment.   For further discussion, see Cretney, Principles of Family Law 4th ed. (1984), pp. 314, 403; Maidment, Child Custody and Divorce (1984), pp. 27-28.

care and control to one party intending to produce identical effects.[117] It is certainly difficult to explain those effects to the parties.

Legal custody

2.40   "Legal custody" is a creature of statute and is the term used, instead of "custody", in all statutory provisions dealing with child custody except those of the 1973 Act.   The Children Act 1975 first defines "the parental rights and duties" and then defines "legal custody" in terms of those rights and duties:

> "85.   (1) In this Act, unless the context otherwise requires, 'the parental rights and duties' means as respects a particular child (whether legitimate or not), all the rights and duties which by law the mother and father have in relation to a legitimate child and his property; and references to a parental right or duty shall be construed accordingly and shall include a right of access and any other element included in a right or duty".

> "86.   In this Act, unless the context otherwise requires, 'legal custody' means, as respects a child, so much of the parental rights and duties as relate to the person of the child (including the place and manner in which his time is spent); but a person shall not by virtue of having legal custody of a child be entitled to effect or arrange for his emigration from the United Kingdom unless he is a parent or guardian of the child."

In any Act, unless the contrary intention appears, the expressions "the parental rights and duties" and "legal custody" are to be construed in accordance with these definitions.[118]

---

117   See the Supplement to this Working Paper: Priest and Whybrow, Custody Law in Practice in the Divorce and Domestic Courts (1986).

118   Interpretation Act 1978, Schedule 1.

2.41   Where a court makes an order for legal custody, this presumably covers all the parental rights and duties which "relate to the person of the child". Certainly the order does not cover rights and duties which do not relate to the person (such as rights over his property)[119] which would be included in the wider, but not the narrower, sense of "custody" described earlier. It is not clear, however, what rights and duties "relate to the person"; and if (as seems likely) they include power to make major decisions regarding the child's upbringing, such as his education or religion,[120] whether the limitations on custody orders stated in Dipper v. Dipper[121] are also applicable to orders for legal custody.

> (Q23) Under the 1973 Act, the courts may award "custody", whereas under the other enactments, they are limited to "legal custody": do these terms require clarification, in particular as to the matters over which the person granted such "custody" or legal custody has sole control?

> (Q24) Should the orders available under the various enactments be made consistent? If so, is "custody" or "legal custody" preferable?   Or is there some other more appropriate concept?

---

119   See Cretney, Principles of Family Law 4th ed. (1984), p. 311; Maidment, "The Fragmentation of Parental Rights" (1981) 40 C.L.J. 135, 138-140; Bevan and Parry, The Children Act 1975 (1979), para. 232.

120   Although at first sight a child's religion might seem to relate to his person (including the place and manner in which his time is spent) it would be surprising if a custodian could change a child's religion when a local authority having parental rights (or powers) and duties is expressly prohibited from doing so: Child Care Act 1980, ss. 4(3) and 10(3).

121   See para. 2.36 above.

Dividing and sharing custody

2.42   As we have already seen, under the 1973 Act the court may order both the dividing and the sharing of the powers and responsibilities contained in "custody".   In the past the more usual form of such orders gave custody to one spouse alone, with care and control to the other.[122] Nowadays, such orders are disapproved and the proper course in appropriate cases is to grant them joint custody, with care and control to one.   As was said in Dipper v. Dipper, " ... care has to be taken not to affront the parent carrying the burden day-to-day of looking after the child by giving custody to the absent parent".[123]   Hence the parent with care and control should not be deprived of a voice in the major decisions in the child's life, even though it may be appropriate for responsibility for those decisions to be shared.   Orders for joint custody are becoming increasingly common, particularly in certain parts of the country, as a means of reflecting and encouraging the continuing concern of both parents for their children's future.[124]   Where the spouses concerned are both parents of the child much the same result can be achieved simply by granting care and control to one parent and leaving the remainder of the "bundle of powers" to be shared according to the Guardianship Act 1973.[125]

---

122   See para. 2.35 and n. 112 above;   Allen v. Allen [1948] 2 All E.R. 413; Wakeham v. Wakeham [1954] 1 W.L.R. 366; Clissold v. Clissold (1964) 108 S.J. 220; Re W. (An Infant) [1964] Ch. 202.

123   Ormrod L.J. at p. 45; for an exceptional case where a "split" order was appropriate, see Jane v. Jane (1983) 4 F.L.R. 712.

124   Report of the Matrimonial Causes Procedure Committee (1985) Chairman: The Honourable Mrs. Justice Booth (the "Booth Report"), paras. 4.130 and 4.131.   See also Jussa v. Jussa [1972] 1 W.L.R. 881.

125   Although there could be a difference between "equal" rights under the Act and "joint" rights under the order: see para. 2.2 above.

2.43   The precise division between those aspects of parental responsibility which are contained in "care and control" and those which are shared in "joint custody" is not entirely clear.   It appears to be generally assumed that long-term decisions, such as the child's religious upbringing and the choice of a school, are contained in joint custody.[126] How far this descends into details, such as regularity of worship or choice of optional subjects, is not known.   Other "major" decisions, perhaps relating to serious medical treatment, may also be included.[127] However, in Dipper v. Dipper[128] itself, Cumming-Bruce L.J. cautioned against "giving the other parent an apparent right to interfere in the day-to-day matters or in the general way in which the parent with care and control intends to lead his or her life".   It seems clear that a joint custody order is not intended to give the other parent that right, but the dividing line between major matters of upbringing and the parent's way of life may be hard to draw, for example when a change of home is planned.

2.44   There are other aspects to the flexibility allowed under the 1973 Act.   Joint custody may be ordered, not between the divorcing spouses, but between one of them and a new step-parent.   Indeed, as already seen, some encouragement towards this course as an alternative to adoption was given by the Children Act 1975.[129]   In such cases, joint custody in law will be accompanied by shared care and control.   It is also possible for the court to order shared care and control, or shared physical custody, where the divorcing spouses each intend to continue to play a large part in the day-to-day care of their child.   This is the sense in

---

126   Cretney, Principles of Family Law 4th ed. (1984), p. 402.

127   In Jane v. Jane (1983) 4 F.L.R. 712, the Court of Appeal assumed consent to serious medical treatment would be included in joint custody.

128   [1981] Fam. 31 at p. 48.

129   C.A. 1975 ss. 10(3) and 11(4): see para. 2.32 above.

which "joint custody" is sometimes meant in the United States.[130] In the past the same result used to be achieved in this country by giving each spouse custody for part of the year.[131]

2.45   This flexibility is not permitted, however, under the other statutory jurisdictions.   Under both the Domestic Proceedings and Magistrates' Courts Act 1978 and all three of the custody jurisdictions in the Guardianship of Minors Act 1971, it is expressly provided that:[132]

> "An order shall not be made ... giving the legal custody of a child to more than one person; but where the court makes an order giving the legal custody of [a child] [a minor] to any person ... it may order that [a party to the marriage in question] [a parent of the minor] who is not given the legal custody of the [child] [minor] shall retain all or such as the court may specify of the parental rights and duties comprised in legal custody (other than the right to the actual custody of the [child] [minor]) and shall have those rights jointly with the person who is given legal custody of the [child] [minor]".

The object of these provisions[133] is to cure both of the defects identified in the old "split order": the person with actual custody is not to be deprived of legal custody, but where some sharing of the parental responsibility is appropriate, it should be made plain exactly what is involved.

---

130   See Miller, "Joint Custody" (1979) 13 F.L.Q. 345; and paras. 4.44-4.46 below.

131   See e.g. Re A. and B. [1897] 1 Ch. 786; see also Marriage Act 1949, Second Schedule.

132   G.M.A. 1971, s. 11A(1); D.P.M.C.A. 1978, s. 8(4).

133   See Law Com. No. 77 (op. cit. at n. 20), paras. 5.23-5.34.

2.46   Nevertheless, there are difficulties.   The court may order that the non-custodial parent (under the 1971 Act) or the other party to the marriage (under the 1978 Act) shall "retain" specified responsibilities. The word "retain" might be taken to imply the retention by a party of rights and duties already held.   More probably it means the retention _for_ a party of rights and duties comprised in legal custody which the court is to distribute, for there would be little purpose in enabling the court to award legal custody to, say, a step-parent but not to award specific rights and duties.   Moreover, in proceedings under the 1978 Act, it may be more appropriate to order the parent who is _not_ a party to the marriage to retain some responsibilities than it is to allow the married party to do so, but the court has no power to do this.

2.47   More importantly, the court may order that the non-custodial parent or party retain "all" the rights and duties comprised in legal custody, apart from the right to actual custody.   This makes it a joint custody order in all but name.   The dividing line between those rights and duties and the right to "actual custody" is no clearer than that between custody and "care and control" under the Matrimonial Causes Act.   In both the 1971 and 1978 Acts, "actual custody" means "actual possession of the person of the child".[134]   This could be more limited than "care and control", which seems to allow a parent to exercise responsibility over all save the most serious and long-term decisions in the child's upbringing.

2.48   It is also unclear whether actual custody may be shared under these enactments.   Where an order granting legal custody is made, such sharing is precluded by the provisions quoted earlier.   However, the court is empowered to make "such order regarding ... the legal custody of the minor ... as the court thinks fit".[135]   If the court under the Matrimonial

---

134   G.M.A. 1971, s. 20(2); D.P.M.C.A. 1978, s. 88(1).

135   G.M.A. 1971, ss. 9(1), 10(1) and 11(a); D.P.M.C.A. 1978, s. 8(2).

Causes Act is entitled to make an order for care and control by virtue of its power to "make such order as it thinks fit for the custody and education of any child of the family", it is difficult to understand why a court cannot similarly make an order for "actual custody" alone under both the 1971 and 1978 Acts. There is some support for this view in the provisions relating to maintenance for the child in both Acts, which refer to an order giving the "right to actual custody".[136] If an order relating to actual custody alone is made, then the prohibition upon giving legal custody to more than one person would not apply, so that it would be possible for actual custody to be shared.

2.49   Under the custodianship provisions of the Children Act 1975, however, the position is quite different. There may be joint custodians and a step-parent custodian may have legal custody jointly with the parent to whom he or she is married.[137] The right of any other person to legal custody is suspended[138] and there is no provision for retaining specified parental rights and duties. Now that these provisions also apply where third parties are granted custody in proceedings under the 1971 and 1978 Acts, the courts have been deprived of the power to award custody to, for example, the grandmother of an illegitimate child while allowing the mother to retain her voice in matters such as education or religion. It seems clear that the only order which can be made is one "vesting legal custody", so that an order for actual custody alone is not possible.[139] Hence, although there may be rather more certainty as to the contents of the orders made, considerably less flexibility is permitted than under the other enactments.

---

136   G.M.A. 1971, s. 9(2); D.P.M.C.A. 1978, ss. 11(1) and (2).

137   C.A. 1975, s. 44(2).

138   C.A. 1975, s. 44(1).

139   C.A. 1975, s. 33(1).

2.50   If a person holds a parental right or duty jointly he may exercise it how he wishes unless another person holding it has signified disapproval.[140]   The 1971, 1975 and 1978 Acts all contain powers where such people cannot agree for either to apply to the court to make such order as it thinks fit.[141]   There is no equivalent in the 1973 Act; if the parties are parents they may resort to section 1(3) of the Guardianship Act 1973;   otherwise the court's powers to deal with "custody" may be sufficient to resolve the matter.

> (Q25) Under the 1973 Act, the courts may award "care and control" to one person; the other parental responsibilities may be shared equally by operation of law or be the subject of a joint custody order: should this remain possible?   If so, does the division of responsibility require clarification?

> (Q26) Does the status of the person who is not awarded care and control, but has powers under a joint custody order or by operation of law require clarification?   In particular, should there be independent powers of action, a power of veto or a duty to consult?

> (Q27) Should it remain possible under the 1973 Act to make "split" orders whereby "care and control" is granted to one person and sole custody to another?

> (Q28) Under the 1971 and 1978 Acts, the courts cannot expressly grant joint legal custody, although they may order the retention of specified parental rights and duties: is this approach preferable to that in the 1973 Act?

---

140   C.A. 1975, s. 85(3).

141   G.M.A. 1971, s. 7;   C.A. 1975, s. 38;   D.P.M.C.A. 1978, s. 13.

(Q29) Should the categories of people who may share specified parental rights and duties under the 1971 and 1978 Acts be extended, in particular to include parents in proceedings under the 1978 Act?

(Q30) Does the division of responsibility between legal and actual custody require clarification?

(Q31) Should it be possible to order that actual custody or care and control be shared under all these enactments?

(Q32) Should it be possible to share parental rights and duties with custodians?

(Q33) Should there be uniform powers to resolve disputed questions between people sharing parental rights and duties?

Other effects of custody orders

Change of name

2.51　　A custody order in proceedings under the 1973 Act must, "unless otherwise directed" provide that no step (other than the institution of proceedings in a court) may be taken by the parent which would result in the child being known by a new surname except with the leave of a judge or the consent in writing of the other parent.[142]　On this question (as on others), the child's welfare is the paramount consideration, and a balance has to be struck between preservation of links with the non-custodial parent and the child's integration into his new family and school environment.[143]　There is no equivalent provision in any other custody

---

142　Matrimonial Causes Rules 1977, r. 92(8).

143　W. v. A. [1981] Fam. 14; Re W.G. (1976) 6 Fam. Law 210; R. v. R. [1977] 1 W.L.R. 1256; D. v. B. (Orse D.) [1979] Fam. 38.

jurisdiction, but it is unlikely that an order for legal custody confers the unilateral right to change the child's name, or even that the court would have power to permit it. There may be custodianship cases, however, in which such a power would be beneficial.

Consent to marriage

2.52   The provisions of the Marriage Act 1949 as to the consents required to the marriage of a 16 or 17 year old child have been described as "outdated and unsatisfactory".[144]   Where there is a custodianship order, the consent of the custodian, and any parent to whom the custodian is married, is required.[145]   Otherwise, the position is set out in the Second Schedule to the Act.   The underlying policy in relation to a legitimate child appears to be that the consent of both parents is required unless one or both have been deprived of the power of consent by virtue of a custody order or agreement or through desertion.   The mother of an illegitimate child retains the power unless deprived of it by a custody order, for example in favour of the father.[146]   It may be unsatisfactory to make entitlement to consent depend upon the difficult question of whether one party has deserted the other.   It may be equally unsatisfactory to make it depend upon the chance of whether a particular type of order or agreement is made upon separation or divorce. Marriage is pre-eminently a long term question of the sort contemplated in Dipper v. Dipper[147] and should be even more important to the child than a change of surname.

---

144   Cretney, Principles of Family Law 4th ed. (1984), p. 16.

145   Marriage Act 1949, s. 3(1).

146   The draft Family Law Reform Bill annexed to Law Com. No. 118 (op. cit. at n. 3) provides that the father's consent is required if he has the rights to actual custody or the right to consent to marry vested in him by court order, but in addition to that of the mother.

147   [1981] Fam. 31; see para. 2.36 above.

Guardianship

2.53   A custody order has no effect upon the right of both parents of a legitimate child either to appoint a testamentary guardian or to act as guardian on the death of the other.[148] A custody order in favour of the father of an illegitimate child confers both rights upon him, provided in the former case that he was still entitled to custody immediately before his death.[149] We raised in our Guardianship paper the questions of whether a parent who has been deprived of custody should remain entitled to appoint a testamentary guardian[150] and of what should happen if disputes about the care of the child arise between a testamentary guardian appointed by deceased custodial parent and the survivor.[151]

2.54   A decree absolute of divorce or a decree of judicial separation may contain a declaration that either spouse is unfit to have custody of the children of the family.[152] The effect of such a declaration upon a parent is that he is not entitled as of right, upon the death of the other, to custody or guardianship of the child.[153] Presumably such a declaration would always be accompanied by an order depriving the unfit parent of custody for the present, but such future deprivations are rarely thought

---

148   See para. 2.54 below.

149   G.M.A. 1971, s. 14(3); the same could apply to an order under the draft Family Law Reform Bill (op. cit. at n. 3) conferring parental rights and duties upon him.

150   Working Paper No. 91, paras. 3.38-3.40.

151   Ibid., paras. 3.30-3.37.

152   M.C.A. 1973, s. 42(3).

153   M.C.A. 1973, s. 42(4).

appropriate.[154] There is no equivalent power in the other jurisdictions. Thus it appears, for example, that upon the death of the custodian the right of the natural parents will revive. Once again, we raised in our Guardianship paper the question of whether it should be possible in private law to deprive a parent of guardianship as well as custody.[155]

> (Q34) Should the effect of custody orders upon the power to change a child's surname, consent to the child's marriage, appoint testamentary guardians, and act as guardian upon the death of the custodial parent, be clarified and made consistent?

F.   The other orders available

Access

2.55   Access is expressly included in references to a parental right or duty, by virtue of the Children Act 1975, and thus also in "legal custody".[156] Similarly, it is expressly included in the term "custody" in the Matrimonial Causes Act 1973.[157] Under the 1973 Act, the court may award access to anyone, whether or not it also makes an order for custody or care and control.[158] Under the Domestic Proceedings and Magistrates' Courts Act 1978, the court may grant access to a party to the marriage in question or to a parent, whether or not it also makes an

---

154   B. v. B. (1976) 3 F.L.R. 187.

155   Working Paper No. 91, para. 4.43.

156   C.A. 1975, ss. 85(1) and 86: see para. 2.40 above.

157   M.C.A. 1973, s. 52(1).

158   M.C.A. 1973, s. 42(1); the court may make such order as it thinks fit: see para. 2.18 above.

order for legal custody,[159] but can only grant access to a grandparent if there is an order for legal custody.[160] Similarly, under the Guardianship of Minors Act 1971, the court may grant access to the mother or father, whether or not it also makes an order for legal custody,[161] but can only grant access to a grandparent if there is an order for custody[162] or one parent is deceased.[163] Although access is part of legal custody, it cannot be severed from legal custody and granted to any other third party in proceedings under the 1978 Act or section 9 of the 1971 Act, for third parties can only acquire legal custody under the custodianship regime,[164] which does not provide for it to be divided. Under the 1971 and 1978 Acts, the court is expressly prohibited from ordering access if the child is in the care of a local authority, whether voluntarily or compulsorily.[165]

2.56   Hence, if custody is awarded with no order as to access, it would appear that the non-custodial parent is deprived of his right to access, even if (as we understand may well be the case) it is intended that he should continue to see the child. This may not strictly be the position where joint custody is awarded by a divorce court, with care and control to one party, but it is common practice for access orders to be made in

---

159   D.P.M.C.A. 1978, s. 8(2)(b).

160   D.P.M.C.A. 1978, s. 14(1).

161   G.M.A. 1971, ss. 9(1)(b), 10(1)(a)(ii) and 11(a)(ii).

162   G.M.A. 1971, s. 14A(1).

163   G.M.A. 1971, s. 14A(2).

164   C.A. 1975, ss. 33 and 34.

165   G.M.A. 1971, s. 14A(4); D.P.M.C.A. 1978, s. 8(7)(b). R.C.C.L. (op. cit. at n. 22) has recommended that the court hearing care proceedings should be able to deal with access in much the same way that a court hearing custody proceedings may do so; see ch. 21.

such cases also. The usual order is for "reasonable" access, to be agreed between the parties:[166] if they cannot agree, however, the court will define it precisely. There is little guidance in the reported cases as to the considerations to be taken into account in deciding what is reasonable. There is also little guidance as to the status of the parent while he is exercising access: in practice, a period of staying access will be akin to temporary care and control, whereas a short visit or outing will carry much less responsibility.[167]

2.57   Access has been judicially described as the "right of the child".[168]   Nevertheless, an access order is in effect an order to the custodial parent to permit the non-custodial parent to exercise his access; we are not aware of any case in which steps have been taken to oblige a non-custodial parent to see his child.   The enforcement of access is known to cause grave difficulties in some cases: the usual remedies for non-compliance with the courts' orders may harm the very person in whose interests the access order has been made.[169]   The possibility of a variation in the custody order may prove a more effective sanction,[170]

---

166   In the study by Maidment (1976) 6 Fam. Law 195 and 236, 89% of access orders were found to be for "reasonable access", and a similarly high percentage of "reasonable access orders" was found in Eekelaar and Clive's study Custody after Divorce (1977), Family Law Studies No. 1, Centre for Socio-Legal Studies, Wolfson College Oxford, para. 5.7. See also L. v. L. (1980) 1 F.L.R. 396 for the advantages of reasonable access orders.

167   See para. 4.51 below.

168   M. v. M. [1973] 2 All E.R. 81, 85 per Wrangham J.

169   The courts are reluctant to order the imprisonment of a custodial parent, e.g. V.P. v. V.P. (1978) 1 F.L.R. 336; P. v. W. [1984] Fam. 32.   See generally on this problem the Booth Report (op. cit. at n. 124), paras. 4.142-3 and Samuels, "Refusal or failure to observe access order - the remedy for the aggrieved party" (1981) 11 Fam. Law. 156.

170   The court considered this measure in V.P. v. V.P. (ibid).

but once again the cure may be worse than the disease. Nevertheless, the view is normally taken that continued contact with both parents is greatly to the benefit of the child and should be secured or preserved if at all possible.[171]

> (Q35) Should it be possible to award access while the child is in the care of a local authority?

> (Q36) Is there a need for guidelines in deciding what access is reasonable?

> (Q37) Is there a need to clarify the responsibilities of the parent while he is exercising access?

> (Q38) Is there a need to clarify either the obligation of one person to permit access or the obligation of the other to exercise it?

> (Q39) Can and should the measures available to enforce access be improved?

Prohibition against removal from the jurisdiction

2.58   In divorce, nullity or judicial separation proceedings, the court has power on the application of petitioner or respondent to order that the child is not to be removed from England and Wales without leave of the court, except on such terms as may be specified in the order, for example

---

171   D. v. M. [1983] Fam. 33, 37 per Ormrod L.J.; Williams v. Williams (1980) 11 Fam. Law 23, per Templeman L.J.; Symington v. Symington (1875) L.R. 2 Sc. Div. 415, 423 per Lord Cairns: "On both sides there ought to be a careful opportunity of access, so that none of the children may grow up without as full knowledge and as full intercourse as the case will admit of with both parents".

where the other party consents or for short holidays.[172]   In cases of
urgency, it may make such an order before proceedings are issued.[173]
Where the court makes a custody order in proceedings under the 1973 Act,
the order must contain such a prohibition "unless otherwise directed",
whether the prohibition is applied for or not.[174]   Where there is a
custody order (including an interim order) under the other enactments, the
courts are empowered, but only on application,[175] to prohibit removal
without leave and to vary or revoke the prohibition.[176] The Children Act
1975 also provides that a person with legal custody is not entitled to
effect or arrange for the child's emigration from the United Kingdom
unless he is a parent or guardian.[177]   Whether or not there is any express
prohibition, under section 1 of the Child Abduction Act 1984, it can be a

---

172   Matrimonial Causes Rules 1977, r. 94(1).

173   L. v. L. [1969] P. 25.

174   Matrimonial Causes Rules 1977, r. 94(2).

175   The parties who can apply are as follows: D.P.M.C.A. 1978, s. 34(3),
      a party to the marriage or parent of the child; G.M.A. 1971, s.
      13A(3), any party to the proceedings in which the order was made;
      C.A. 1975, s. 43A(3), a parent of the child or the custodian.

176   G.M.A. 1971, s. 13A; C.A. 1975, s. 43A; D.P.M.C.A. 1978, s. 34.
      Law Com. No. 77 (op. cit. at n. 20), para. 10.8 did not consider that
      a prohibition order should be the general rule in custody cases in
      Magistrates' Courts.

177   C.A. 1975, s. 86.   The Law Commission and the Scottish Law
      Commission in Custody of Children - Jurisdiction and Enforcement
      within the United Kingdom (1985) Law Com. No. 138, Scot. Law
      Com. No. 91, para. 6.17 recommended that all courts in each part
      of the United Kingdom which have power to order that a child
      should not be taken from that part should be empowered to order
      that the child should not be taken from the United Kingdom as a
      whole.

criminal offence for one parent to take a child under 16 abroad without the consent of the other or the leave of a court.[178]

2.59   Clearly, the grant of leave to take the child abroad for a long time can have a serious effect upon the links between the child and his other parent.   Nevertheless, the courts have generally taken the view that this alone is not a sufficient reason to interfere with a reasonable way of life which the custodial parent has chosen to adopt.[179]

> (Q40) Should the courts' powers to prohibit removal from the jurisdiction be retained, now that the matter is usually covered by the Child Abduction Act 1984?   If so should they be made consistent?

Supervision orders

2.60   All the enactments conferring custody jurisdiction, save sections 10(1) and 11(a) of the Guardianship of Minors Act 1971, enable the court, if it grants legal custody or (under the 1973 Act) care of the child to any person also to make an order that the child is to be under the supervision of a local authority or a probation officer.   This can be done "if it appears to the court that there are exceptional circumstances which make it desirable that the child should be under the supervision of an independent person".[180]

---

178   For the new procedure for stopping children from actually being removed, see Practice Direction of 14 April 1986, [1986] 1 W.L.R. 475.

179   Poel v. Poel [1970] 1 W.L.R. 1469, 1473 per Sachs L.J.; Barnes v. Tyrrell (1981) 3 F.L.R. 240; Chamberlain v. De La Mare (1982) 4 F.L.R. 434.

180   M.C.A. 1973, s. 44(1); D.P.M.C.A. 1978, s. 9; G.A. 1973, s. 2(2)(a); C.A. 1975, s. 34(5).

2.61   The court is obliged to make a supervision order on revoking a custodianship order, if it is desirable both that the child should be in the legal custody of the person who would be entitled to it on revocation and also in the interests of the child's welfare for him to be under the supervision of an independent person.[181]

2.62   Apart from the Matrimonial Causes Act 1973 the enactments provide that a supervision order ceases to have effect when the child attains eighteen.[182] The courts however have power to vary and revoke supervision orders,[183] and have acted on the assumption that an order may be made for a limited period.[184] The Booth Report has recommended that as a matter of practice supervision orders should normally be made for a defined period,[185] and the Review of Child Care Law has suggested that orders might last for a set period of, say, one year unless the court specifies a shorter or longer term.[186]

2.63   The enactments are silent as to any duties or powers conferred by a supervision order,[187] except that the supervisor may apply for

---

181   C.A. 1975, s. 36(3)(b).

182   D.P.M.C.A. 1978, s. 9(3); G.A. 1973, s. 3(2); C.A. 1975, s. 34(5).

183   M.C.A. 1973, s. 44(5); D.P.M.C.A. 1978, ss. 21(1)(b) and 7(b); G.A. 1973, s. 3(3); C.A. 1975, s. 34(5).

184   (1981) 145 J.P.N. 137.

185   Para. 4.139 (op. cit. at n. 124).

186   R.C.C.L. (op. cit. at n. 22), para. 18.26.

187   See Cretney, Principles of Family Law 4th ed. (1984), p. 404. See also Booth Report (op. cit. at n. 124), para. 4.140 and R.C.C.L. (ibid.), para. 18.27.

variation or revocation[188] and if the order is made under the Matrimonial Causes Act 1973 he may apply for directions as to the exercise of his powers under the order,[189] for variation of custody or access arrangements, or for the child to be committed to care.[190] The Review of Child Care Law has suggested that the supervisor's duty might be clarified as being to "advise, assist and befriend" the child and his parents, and that D.H.S.S. might be given power to make regulations defining further how the local authority should carry out the supervision.[191] It also recommends that supervisors appointed in all proceedings should have the power to apply for variation of the custody or access orders or for committal to care.[192]

2.64   Both the Booth Report[193] and the Review of Child Care Law[194] consider that it would be helpful for the order to state the purpose for which it was made and what it is hoped that supervision will achieve. The Review also considered that it might be advantageous if the court could attach the same requirements as in orders made in care proceedings, addressed to either parent or to the child.[195] At present, in

---

188   M.C.A. 1973, s. 44(5); D.P.M.C.A. 1978, s. 21(7)(b); G.A. 1973, s. 3(3); C.A. 1975, s. 34(5).

189   See Matrimonial Causes Rules 1977, r. 93(4). See R.C.C.L. (op. cit. at n. 22), para. 18.29.

190   See Matrimonial Causes Rules 1977, r. 92(3). See R.C.C.L. (op. cit. at n. 22), para. 18.29.

191   Para. 18.27.

192   Para. 18.29.

193   Para. 4.140.

194   Para. 18.27.

195   Paras. 18.9 and 18.27.

both care and custody proceedings, it is the child who is under supervision and in custody proceedings there is no express power to impose requirements upon him. There is no power at all to impose requirements upon the parents or other parties.

(Q41) Do the circumstances in which supervision orders may be made, or the grounds for them, require amendment?

(Q42) Should a supervision order be for a limited period of, say, one year, unless the court specifies otherwise?

(Q43) Should the duties or powers conferred by a supervision order be clarified?

(Q44) Should the supervisor have power to apply for directions as to the exercise of his powers, for variation of the custody or access arrangements, or for committal to care?

(Q45) Should the court state the purpose for which a supervision order is made?

(Q45A) Should the court have power to impose specific requirements upon the parents or the child?

Committal to local authority care

2.65   All of the enactments conferring custody jurisdiction, apart from sections 10(1) and 11(a) of the Guardianship of Minors Act 1971, enable the court, instead of making a custody order, to make an order committing the child to the care of the local authority.[196]   This

---

196   M.C.A. 1973, s. 43; D.P.M.C.A. 1978, s. 10; G.A. 1973, ss. 2(2)(b) and 4; C.A. 1975, s. 34(5).

jurisdiction is exercisable if the child is under seventeen and "if it appears to the court that there are exceptional circumstances making it impracticable or undesirable" for the child to be entrusted to a parent or other individual. The court is <u>obliged</u> to make a committal order on revoking a custodianship order, if either there is no one who would be entitled to legal custody of the child or it would not be desirable in the interests of the child's welfare for the person who would be entitled to legal custody to have it.[197]

2.66   The courts have power to vary[198] and revoke these orders;[199] if the order is not revoked it continues to have effect until the child attains eighteen.[200]   The order cannot be made for a limited duration.[201]

2.67   These orders do not have the effect of transferring parental rights and duties to the local authority, although the parents cannot

---

197   C.A. 1975, ss. 36(2) and 36(3)(a).

198   The power to vary seems to be a limited one, since the committal to care has the effect of applying the statutory provisions of the Child Care Act 1980.   Possibly the power is linked to the separate power to give directions.   See para. 2.67 below.

199   M.C.A. 1973, s. 43(7);   D.P.M.C.A. 1978, s. 21(1)(c) (revocation only);   G.A. 1973, s. 4(3A);   C.A. 1975, ss. 34(5) and 36(3).

200   M.C.A. 1973, s. 43(4);   D.P.M.C.A. 1978, s. 10(6).   There are no corresponding provisions in the Guardianship Acts or the Children Act 1975, but the terms "minor" and "child" presumably have this effect.

201   R.C.C.L. (<u>op. cit.</u> at n. 22) recommends that in care proceedings (including proceedings for the discharge of a care order) the court should have the power to order a phased return of the child to his family (see paras. 19.6 and 20.26).

remove the child while the order is in force.[202]   The local authority has most of the powers which it would have if it had received the child into voluntary care,[203] but if the order is made under the Matrimonial Causes Act 1973 or in the High Court under the Guardianship of Minors Act 1971 or the Children Act 1975, the exercise of some of these powers is subject to directions given by the court.[204]

2.68   The Review of Child Care Law has recommended that the grounds for, and effects of committal to care in custody proceedings should be the same as in care proceedings,[205] but has asked the Commission to consider the procedures to be adopted, including those for representing the child when such orders are contemplated.[206]

---

202   C.f. M.C.A. 1973, s. 43(3), D.P.M.C.A. 1978, s. 10(5); G.A. 1973, s. 4(5) and C.A. 1975, s. 34(5) with Child Care Act 1980, s. 10(2) under which the local authority has the powers and duties of a parent or guardian where the child has been committed to the authority's care in care proceedings under the Children and Young Persons Act 1969.

203   M.C.A. 1973, ss. 43(1) and (5)(a); D.P.M.C.A. 1978, s. 10(4)(a); G.A. 1973, s. 4(4); C.A. 1975 ss. 34(5) and 36(6).

204   Under M.C.A. 1973, s. 43(5)(a), directions may apply to the local authorities' powers under ss. 18, 21 and 22 of the Child Care Act 1980 which define the authorities' general duties (s. 18), the duty to provide accommodation and maintenance (s. 21) and duties regarding the boarding out of children (s. 22).   Under G.A. 1973, s. 4(4)(a), directions may apply to ss. 18 and 21.   C.A. 1975, ss. 34(5) and 36(6), adopt G.A. 1973, s. 4.

205   R.C.C.L. (op. cit. at n. 22), para. 15.35;   this would result in the courts losing the power to give directions mentioned in para. 2.67.

206   Ibid., para. 14.18.

(Q46) Should the grounds for, and effects of, committal to care in the course of custody proceedings be the same as those in care proceedings? In particular, should the High Court and courts acting under the 1973 Act retain the power to give directions to the local authority?

(Q47) Should the procedures for committal to care be the same as those in care proceedings?

Wardship and transfer to the High Court

2.69 In proceedings for divorce, nullity or judicial separation the court has power, instead of making a custody order, to "direct that proper proceedings be taken for making the child a ward of the court".[207] There is no equivalent in the other jurisdictions. A county court may, either of its own motion, or on the application of any party to the proceedings, order the transfer of family proceedings to the High Court.[208] The High Court may similarly order the transfer of family proceedings to,[209] or from,[210] a county court. There is no provision for the transfer of cases from magistrates' domestic courts, but the court can refuse to hear any matter which would more conveniently be dealt with by the High

---

207 M.C.A. 1973, s. 42(1). The power is rarely used. It is unusual in giving the court the initiative to open new proceedings, but its purpose appears to be to enable the court to retain control over the child.

208 Matrimonial and Family Proceedings Act (M.F.P.A.) 1984, s. 39(1). Section 37 gives the President of the Family Division power to give directions on the transfer of family proceedings between county courts and the High Court.

209 M.F.P.A. 1984, s. 38(1).

210 County Courts Act 1984, s. 41.

Court,[211] to which a new application must then be made.

(Q48) In what circumstances should it be possible for any court hearing custody proceedings to direct that the child be made a ward of court or otherwise transfer the case to the High Court?

G.   Ancillary matters

Interim orders

2.70   There is no specific provision in the Matrimonial Causes Act 1973 for the making of interim orders (i.e. temporary orders pending the full hearing or the completion of negotiations), but it is clear that they can be made under the powers conferred by section 42.[212] The 1978 Act gives a domestic court power to make an interim order at any time before finally disposing of the case, but only if there are "special circumstances" making this desirable.[213]   Similar provision is made for applications under section 9 (but not sections 10(1) and 11(a)) of the Guardianship of Minors Act 1971,[214] and this is also applied to applications for custodianship.[215]

2.71   There is no limit in the 1973 Act upon the number or duration of interim orders.   The other Acts contain uniform provisions whereby the court cannot make more than one interim order in relation to each

---

211   G.M.A. 1971, s. 16(4); C.A. 1975, s. 101(3); D.P.M.C.A. 1978, s. 27.

212   See Rayden on Divorce 14th ed. (1983), p. 1064.

213   D.P.M.C.A. 1978, s. 19.

214   G.A. 1973, s. 2(4).

215   C.A. 1975, s. 34(5) applies the provisions of G.A. 1973, s. 2(4).

original application[216] and an interim order ordinarily ceases to have effect not later than three months after it is made[217] but may be continued by order for a further period of not more than three months.[218] Allowing such interim orders to run indefinitely was rejected on the grounds that an interim order is no substitute for an order made in substantive proceedings and might encourage unreasonable delay.[219] It is in the child's interests that the uncertainties about his future should be settled as soon as possible, and there is evidence that the resolution of contested custody in divorce cases can take a very long time.[220] This may therefore, be one respect in which the approach of the other legislation is to be preferred.

> (Q49) Should it be possible to make interim orders under the 1971, 1975 or 1978 Acts otherwise than in "special circumstances"?

> (Q50) Should the time limits upon interim orders under those Acts be abolished or made applicable also under the 1973 Act?

Non-removal provisions in custodianship

2.72   The Children Act 1975 prohibits the removal of a child from certain people who are applying for custodianship. Where a person with

---

216   G.A. 1973, s. 2(5E); D.P.M.C.A. 1978, s. 19(7); C.A. 1975, s. 34(5).

217   G.A. 1973, s. 2(5C); D.P.M.C.A. 1978, s. 19(5); C.A. 1975, s. 34(5).

218   G.A. 1973, s. 2(5D); D.P.M.C.A. 1978, s. 19(6); C.A. 1975, s. 34(5).

219   Law Com. No. 77 (op. cit. at n. 20), para. 4.32.

220   See Eekelaar and Clive (op. cit. at n. 166), Table 18, which shows that in contested cases the time from the divorce petition to the custody settlement was over six months in 91.1% of cases and over a year in 46.7% of cases.

whom a child has had his home for a total of three years applies for a custodianship order in respect of that child, no one is allowed to remove the child from that person's home without his consent or the leave of the court.[221] This rule applies to a local authority which has placed the child with a foster parent.[222] There are criminal sanctions for its breach[223] and the court has power to order the return of a child who has been removed[224] and to make an order forbidding a threatened breach.[225] There is no equivalent in the other jurisdictions, save for the provisions relating to removal from the country which have already been mentioned.[226]

(Q51) Is there a case for extending the non-removal provisions in custodianship to other circumstances?

Conditional orders

2.73   The courts' powers under the Matrimonial Causes Act 1973 are wide enough to include the power to make conditional orders (i.e. orders subject to the occurrence of some event or the expiration of some period). The other enactments contain express provisions[227] whereby the court may direct that an interim or final custody order is not to have effect until the occurrence of an event, or the expiration of a period (or further period), specified by the court.

---

221   C.A. 1975, s. 41(1).

222   C.A. 1975, s. 41(2).

223   C.A. 1975, s. 41(3).

224   C.A. 1975, s. 42(1).

225   C.A. 1975, s. 42(2).

226   See para. 2.58 above.

227   D.P.M.C.A. 1978, ss. 8(6) and 19(4);   G.M.A. 1971, ss. 11A(2) and 14A(3): G.A. 1973, s. 2(5A);   C.A. 1975, ss. 34(5) and 37(4A).

(Q52) Should the power to make conditional orders under the 1973 Act be made express and consistent with that under the other enactments?

Variation and revocation of orders

2.74　　　　In general, any order for custody or access may be varied or revoked by the court which made it, and most of the enactments contain express provisions to this effect.[228]　　There is no provision in the 1975 Act for the variation of a custodianship order.　The original order must be revoked and a new one made in favour of a qualified applicant.[229]

2.75　　　　Generally only parties to the proceedings may apply for variation or revocation of the order.　However:

(a)　　anyone may intervene for this purpose in proceedings under the 1973 Act, although some will need leave;[230]

228　M.C.A. 1973, s. 42(7) (which also enables the court to suspend the provisions of an order and revive the suspended provisions); D.P.M.C.A. 1978, s. 21(1)(a) and (3) and s. 14(3); G.M.A. 1971, ss. 9(4), 10(2), 11(c) and s. 14A(5) and (6), and G.A. 1973, s. 5(2).　The distinction between a variation of an existing order and the making of a new order is not always clear.　Perhaps the commonest case of variation is where access is subsequently granted or its terms are altered.　Where the court transfers custody from one party to the other it might be thought that it is in effect making a new order. This seems to be the implication of D.P.M.C.A. 1978, s. 21(1) which enables the court on an application for variation of a custody order under s. 8, to make "such other order ... under section 8 as it thinks fit".　Similarly, G.M.A. 1971, s. 10(2) gives a power to make a custody order "at any time".

229　The order may however be varied by making an access order, which is variable: C.A. 1975, s. 35(3) and (4).

230　See para. 2.18 and n. 51 above.

(b)   a parent who is not a party to the marriage in question may apply to vary or revoke a custody or access (including a grandparent's access) order made under the 1978 Act;[231]

(c)   a guardian may apply to vary or revoke a custody or access order made under section 9(1) of the 1971 Act and also an access order made in favour of a grandparent after the death of a parent;[232] the same applies to a third party granted legal custody under that Act;

(d)   a custodianship order may be revoked upon the application of the custodian, the mother or father of the child, or any local authority.[233]

(Q53) Are the provisions as to revocation or variation of, or substitution of new, orders acceptable?

Duration of orders

2.76   A custody order cannot continue in effect after the child's eighteenth birthday.[234] There are also certain special provisions for cessation:

---

231   D.P.M.C.A. 1978, ss. 21(7) and 14(3).

232   G.M.A. 1971, ss. 9(4), 14(A)(6).

233   C.A. 1975, s. 35(1).

234   D.P.M.C.A. 1978, ss. 8(5) and 14(2); G.M.A. 1971, s. 11A(3); C.A. 1975, s. 35(6); see also M.C.A. s. 42(1), (2) and (6).

(a) a custody order made in conjunction with an order for financial provision under section 27 of the 1973 Act has effect "only as respects any period when an order is in force" under that section[235] and thus not, presumably, where the order is for a lump sum which has been paid; however, financial provision may be ordered for the applicant spouse or a child and as long as there is such an order, any person may have custody;

(b) where actual custody is given to one of the spouses by an order (including an interim order) under the 1978 Act, or to one of the parents under the 1971 Act, the order ceases to have effect if they continue to live together, or resume living together, for a continuous period of more than six months;[236] there is no equivalent provision in the 1973 Act;

(c) an access order for grandparents made in conjunction with an order for legal custody under either the 1971 Act or the 1978 Act ceases to have effect if the principal order ceases to have effect, and any order for access made in conjunction with a custodianship order ceases to have effect if the custodianship order is revoked.[237]

---

235 M.C.A. 1973, s. 42(2).

236 D.P.M.C.A. 1978, s. 25(1); G.A. 1973, s. 5A(1). These provisions were recommended in Law Com. No. 77 (op. cit. at n. 20), paras. 5.109 and 6.33 on the basis that where the parents are cohabiting the order is of no practical utility.

237 D.P.M.C.A. 1978, s. 14(5); G.M.A. 1971, s. 14A(8); C.A. 1975, s. 35(5).

(Q54) Should a custody order made in conjunction with an application for financial provision under the 1973 Act have effect irrespective of whether an order for such provision is in force?

(Q55) Should the provisions for cessation of orders where the parties or parents live together for more than six months be abolished or made applicable also under the 1973 Act?

(Q56) Should access orders in favour of grandparents continue in force whether or not the original custody order is still in effect?

Overlapping orders

2.77 A magistrates' court cannot make an order for custody or access under the 1978 Act if there is in force a custody order relating to the same child made by any court in England and Wales.[238] There are no equivalent provisions in any of the other enactments, so that in theory any court has jurisdiction to make an order which supersedes a previous order of either a higher or lower court.[239] However, it has been held that, although there is jurisdiction to do so, a magistrates' court should not make an adoption order which is inconsistent with a custody order made in a higher court[240] and it seems probable that a similar restraint should be

---

238 D.P.M.C.A. 1978, s. 8(7)(a).

239 Certainly a later order by a divorce court supersedes an earlier order under the 1971 or 1978 Acts, see Practice Note, 18 June 1975, Rayden on Divorce 14th ed. (1983), p. 3913-3914. Where a lower court has a new basis of jurisdiction its orders can supersede those of a higher court; see Law Com. No. 138, Scot. Law Com. No. 91 (op. cit. at n. 177), para. 4.115.

240 Re B. [1975] Fam. 127, 142.

exercised in relation to custody. In the Children Act 1975, however, it is expressly provided that a custodianship order will suspend the right of any other person to legal custody, which right will revive if the custodianship order is revoked.[241] Clearly, therefore, there is jurisdiction to make an order which is inconsistent with a custody order made by another, possibly higher, court, although once again restraint may be exercised in practice. The 1975 Act also gives jurisdiction, inter alia to magistrates' courts, to make or vary access orders or to revoke custodianship orders made in other courts.[242]

2.78   Similarly, it is clear that a custodianship order will suspend rather than supersede a care order made under the Children and Young Persons Act 1969.[243] The effect of custody orders made under the other enactments is less clear.   A custody order may be made under the 1978 Act while a child is in care,[244] but the effect is probably to determine who is to have custody when the care order is discharged, rather than to supersede the care order itself.[245] The same may be true, at least for

---

241   C.A. 1975, s. 44(1).

242   C.A. 1975, s. 100(7).

243   Any parental powers and duties not contained in legal custody will remain with the local authority, as is also the case where an authority has assumed parental rights by resolution under s. 3, Child Care Act 1980.

244   M. v. Humberside County Council [1979] Fam. 114, 119.

245   Horsman, "Custody Orders for Children in Care" (1979) 143 J.P. 517; Lowe, "Wardship or Custody for Children in Care" (1980) 43 M.L.R. 586.

magistrates' courts, under the 1971 Act.[246] There is authority, however, that a divorce court, like the High Court, may in exceptional circumstances make a custody order which will supersede an existing care order and thus remove the child from compulsory care.[247]

2.79   As we have already mentioned,[248] the Review of Child Care Law has recommended that a court hearing care proceedings or discharging a care order should have power to make a custody order. It was clearly contemplated that, just as a care order may be inconsistent with a custody order made previously in another court, so might a custody order made in care proceedings be inconsistent with a custody order made, for example, on divorce.

> (Q56A) In what circumstances should one court have power to make custody (or other) orders inconsistent with orders made in another?

> (Q56B) What should be the effect of such orders? Should they supersede or merely suspend the order with which they are inconsistent?

---

246   It is unlikely that the 1971 Act could be used so as to appeal against a care order. In A. v. Liverpool City Council [1982] A.C. 362 and Re W. [1985] A.C. 791 the House of Lords declared that the wardship jurisdiction was not to be used so as to supervise the exercise of discretion within the field committed by statute to local authorities. The same policy would probably apply to the 1971 Act. However there are situations where a custody order could be made. For example in R. v. Oxford Justices ex parte H. [1974] 2 All E.R. 356 it was held that the father of an illegitimate child could apply under the 1971 Act for custody of a child in respect of whom the local authority had assumed the mother's parental rights under s. 3 of the Child Care Act 1980.

247   E. v. E. and Cheshire County Council No. 2 (1979) 1 F.L.R. 73; normally, however, an order would have the same effect as under other enactments; see H. v. H. [1973] Fam. 62.

248   Para. 2.7 above.

H. Who represents the child?

2.80   In custody proceedings, the parties are almost always the adults involved and the interests of the child must for the most part be ascertained from the evidence which they put before the court. However, in some cases, the child may be separately represented or be made a full party to the proceedings; and it is almost always open to the court to call for an independent welfare officer's report.

2.81   Both the High Court and the county court have power to direct that the child be made a party.[249] The Court of Appeal has said that in many cases this is unnecessary, particularly where a child is not old enough to express a view as to his future, and that children should not be made parties unless there are special reasons for doing so.[250] A child who is a party will always have a guardian ad litem who must act through a solicitor.[251] In proceedings under the 1973 Act, however, the court may appoint a guardian ad litem for any child who ought to be separately represented, without making the child a party.[252] A guardian ad litem under these rules may be the Official Solicitor or any other proper person (provided in each case that he consents). There is no provision for the child to become a party or be separately represented in magistrates' domestic courts.[253]

---

249 R.S.C. O.90, r. 6(1); C.C.R. 0.15, r. 1 (which attracts the provisions of R.S.C. O.15, r. 6).

250 P. v. P. (1981) [1982] C.L.Y. 452; Re F. (1982) 3 F.L.R. 101, Re C. [1984] F.L.R. 419; Practice Direction, 8 December 1981 [1982] 1 W.L.R. 118.

251 R.S.C. 0.80, r. 2(1) and (6); C.C.R. 0.10, r. 1(2).

252 Matrimonial Causes Rules 1977, r. 115(1), (2).

253 The question of child representation in magistrates' courts was considered in Law Com. No. 77 (op. cit. at n. 20), paras. 10.25 - 10.36. However, no recommendations for such representation were made because it was considered that it would involve an unacceptably heavy burden on welfare services, and because Parliament had just given the matter "very full consideration" in debating the Children Bill (which became the Children Act 1975).

2.82   These rules apply even where it is contemplated that the child be committed to the care of a local authority.   In care proceedings under the Children and Young Persons Act 1969, on the other hand, the child is invariably a party and entitled to legal representation;   in some cases there will also be a guardian ad litem, from a panel of specialists set up under the Children Act 1975.[254]   The child may also be made a party to proceedings under the Child Care Act 1980 relating to the assumption of parental rights by resolution or to the denial of access to his parents.[255] The Review of Child Care Law has recommended that consideration be given to applying the same provisions where committal to care is contemplated in custody proceedings;[256]   this obviously raises the question of whether any distinction can or should be made depending upon the type of order sought.

2.83   In most proceedings in which a custody order may be made, the court may call for a welfare report, in proceedings under the 1973 Act from the Court Welfare Officer and in other cases from a Probation Officer or the local social services authority.[257]   The exceptions are disputes between parents and guardians under the 1971 Act,[258] applications relating to the removal of a child from the jurisdiction under the 1971 or 1978 Acts where these are made after the custody order has been made,[259] applications for the variation or revocation of a care order

---

254   Children and Young Persons Act 1969, ss. 32A and 32B, inserted by Children Act 1975; see also 1975 Act, s. 103.

255   Child Care Act 1980, ss. 7 and 12F.

256   Para. 14.18 (op. cit. at n. 22).

257   D.P.M.C.A. 1978, ss. 12(3), (4), (5), (6), (7), 13(3), 14(4) and 21(5); Matrimonial Causes Rules 1977, r. 95; C.A. 1975, s. 39; G.A. 1973, s. 6; G.M.A. 1971, s. 14A(7).

258   G.M.A. 1971, ss. 4(4) and 7.

259   G.M.A. 1971, s. 13A; D.P.M.C.A. 1978, s. 34.

under the 1971 Act[260] and (probably) applications for an interim custody order under the 1978 Act.[261]

2.84   The criterion for ordering a welfare report is not identical in all cases.   Under the 1973 Act the court "may at any time refer to a court welfare officer for investigation and report any matter arising in matrimonial proceedings which concerns the welfare of a child".[262] Under the 1971 and 1975 Acts the court may order a report "with respect to any specified matter ... appearing relevant to the application".[263] Under the 1978 Act, a similar criterion applies, but the power is only exercisable "when the court ... is of the opinion that it has not sufficient information" to exercise its powers.[264]

2.85   In custodianship applications, in addition to the court's discretionary powers the local social services authority must always be notified and prepare a report on the matters prescribed by regulation[265] and any other matter which seems relevant.[266]   Before revoking a custodianship order the court must unless it has sufficient information call for a report, from a probation officer or the local authority, on the desirability of the child returning to the legal custody of any individual.[267]

---

260   G.A. 1973, s. 2(2)(b).

261   D.P.M.C.A. s. 12(3); the power of the court to order a report is for deciding "whether to exercise its powers under sections 8 to 10".

262   Matrimonial Causes Rules, r. 95(1).

263   G.A. 1973, s. 6(1); C.A. 1975, s. 39(1).

264   D.P.M.C.A. 1978, s. 12(3).

265   The Custodianship (Reports) Regulations 1985 (S.I. No. 792 amended by S.I. 1985 No. 1494).

266   C.A. 1975, s. 40.

267   C.A. 1975, s. 36(4).

2.86   A judge in proceedings in the High Court or county court may interview the child in private, although care must be taken to observe the rules of natural justice.[268]   Magistrates have no power to interview the child and in most cases it may be thought preferable for the child's views to be sought and put before the court by means of the welfare officer's report.[269]   It appears that this is also generally thought preferable to ordering separate representation for the child.[270]

> (Q57) Should it be possible in all proceedings either to make the child a party or to order that he be separately represented?

> (Q58) If so, should the criteria for making such orders be specified?

> (Q59) If the child becomes a party or is separately represented, should this entail both a guardian ad litem and a lawyer?

> (Q60) If the court is contemplating committing the child to care, should the provisions relating to the representation of the child be the same as those in care proceedings?

---

268   See e.g. Re K. [1963] Ch. 381, 406, 411.

269   In his evidence to the House of Commons' Social Services Committee (Children in Care p. 595), Sir John Arnold P. said he would like to see a change in the law to enable magistrates to interview children in private. However, in Law Com. No. 77 (op. cit. at n. 20), paras. 10.37-10.43, it was thought that magistrates should not be able to interview the children: it would mean the child being interviewed by three justices and a justices' clerk which would be intimidating and a magistrate might find greater difficulty than a judge in deciding what course to adopt so as to ensure fairness to all parties.   It considered that magistrates could adequately discover the child's wishes from a social worker.

270   Law Com. No. 77 (ibid.), para. 10.36; see also Practice Direction, 8 December 1981 [1982] 1 W.L.R. 118.

(Q61) Is there a case for extending those provisions, if not to all custody proceedings, at least to custodianship?

(Q62) Should the courts have the same power to call for a welfare officer's report in all proceedings?

(Q63) Should the courts have greater powers to seek information on their own initiative, for example, by interviewing the child or calling witnesses?

I.   The criteria for custody decisions

2.87   Section 1 of the Guardianship of Minors Act 1971 is as follows:-

"Where in any proceedings before any court (whether or not a court as defined in section 15 of this Act) -

(a)   the legal custody or upbringing of a minor; or

(b)   the administration of any property belonging to or held on trust for a minor, or the application of the income thereof,

"is in question, the court, in deciding that question, shall regard the welfare of the minor as the first and paramount consideration, and shall not take into consideration whether from any other point of view the claim of the father, in respect of such legal custody, upbringing, administration or application is superior to that of the mother, or the claim of the mother is superior to that of the father."

2.88   Although this provision (commonly called "the welfare principle") appears to apply to all the jurisdictions under review here[271] some of the enactments conferring custody jurisdiction expressly attract it,[272] and the custody provisions of the Guardianship of Minors Act 1971 itself (sections 9, 10 and 11) also require the court to "have regard to the welfare of the minor".   Moreover it is not strictly applicable to certain orders made after a custodianship order is revoked: as we have seen,[273] there are circumstances in which the court, on revoking a custodianship order, is obliged to make a supervision order or a care order, and this is so whether or not the welfare of the child is best served by an order in favour of some individual.

2.89   The majority of the enactments provide no other criterion by which questions concerning custody are to be decided.   However, in the particular case of an application by a parent under section 9(1) of the Guardianship of Minors Act 1971 the court is also required to "have regard to the conduct and wishes of the mother and father".[274]   By contrast, in adoption cases, the courts are required to ascertain the child's own wishes and feelings, insofar as this is practicable, and give due consideration to them, having regard to his age and understanding.[275]

---

271   Presumably the principle applies in adoption proceedings for the purpose of interim or final custody orders (see paras. 2.31-2.32 above and Bevan and Parry, The Children Act 1975 (1979) para. 274, although the principle applied "in reaching any decision relating to the adoption of the child" is to "have regard to all the circumstances, first consideration being given to the need to safeguard and promote the welfare of the child through his childhood" (Children Act 1975, s. 3)).   For a discussion of the principle in adoption, see Cretney, Principles of Family Law 4th ed. (1984), pp. 426-428.

272   D.P.M.C.A. 1978, s. 15; C.A. 1975, s. 33(9).

273   See para. 2.61 above.

274   This inconsistency would be removed were the amendments to the 1971 Act recommended in our Report on Illegitimacy, Law Com. No. 118 (op. cit. at n. 3), to be enacted.

275   C.A. 1975, s. 3.

(Q64) Should the criteria applicable to custody decisions be the same in all cases?

(Q65) Is there a need for greater guidance in the application of the "welfare principle"?

(Q66) In particular, should the court be required to ascertain and consider the child's own wishes and feelings?

J. Conclusion

2.90   This discussion has raised a great many questions on which there is doubt or criticism or where the existing statutory provisions are inconsistent with one another.   This in itself presents, in our view, an unanswerable case for reform.   However, both consistency and the resolution of doubts and criticisms could be achieved without collecting all the relevant provisions into a single code.   We shall examine the arguments for and against such a code in Part VII.   To some extent, however, the answer to that question, as to many of the others posed here, depends upon the answers to some more fundamental questions, about the nature of the courts' role in monitoring the welfare of children whose parents separate or are divorced, about the orders which should be available between them, and about the circumstances in which non-parents should be able to seek or be granted similar orders relating to other people's children.   It is to those questions which we now turn.

PART III

THE OBJECTIVES OF A CUSTODY LAW

3.1   As we said earlier, our objective is not only to rationalise and simplify the law but also to ensure that it accords as best it can with the "first and paramount consideration" of the children's welfare.   This is already the law, once any question relating to custody or upbringing has to be decided by a court.[1]   As we shall see in Part VI, the welfare principle was adopted during the gradual process of according equal status to the mothers of legitimate children and would seem the obvious means of resolving disputes between people whose claims might otherwise be thought identical.   Even so, operating the principle is no easy matter, for it involves making value judgments as to the best outcome for a particular child and predictions as to what course will achieve it.

3.2   However, the "welfare principle" is not the only relevant criterion even under the present law.   There is some suggestion that parents and others are expected to apply it when making decisions about a child's upbringing.[2]   Of course, they can only be expected to do so among the available alternatives: the best may not be available to them or only available at considerable cost to others.   Further, in many matters of day-to-day living, it is simply not practicable to expect parents always to give priority to their children's interests.   A more realistic criterion might be that laid down for local authorities in the exercise of their

---

1   Guardianship of Minors Act 1971, s. 1; first enacted as Guardianship of Infants Act 1925, s. 1; see further Part VI.

2   Gillick v. West Norfolk and Wisbech Area Health Authority [1986] A.C. 112, at pp. 173 and 184.

parental responsibilities towards children in care:[3] to give first consideration to the need to safeguard and promote the welfare of the child throughout his childhood, and where practicable to ascertain the child's own "wishes and feelings" and give due consideration to them, having regard to his age and understanding.

3.3   Nevertheless, if parents fall short even of this standard, the State (in the shape of a local authority) will usually interfere only if the child is neglected, ill-treated or beyond their control.[4] It is generally accepted that the State should not intervene between parent and child simply because it could provide or arrange something better than the parents can provide, but only if the parents are falling so far below an acceptable standard that their children are suffering harm as a result.[5]

3.4   We must also have in mind the increasing recognition given by the law to the point of view of the child himself, not only in the statutory principle mentioned earlier, but also in decisions culminating in that of the House of Lords in Gillick v. West Norfolk and Wisbech Area Health Authority.[6] If custody is a "dwindling right"[7] which gives way to the child's own capacity to make up his mind, then the court may also have to recognise this when allocating custody between the adults.[8]

---

3   Child Care Act 1980, s. 18(1); see also Review of Child Care Law ("R.C.C.L.") (1985), para. 2.18.

4   Children and Young Persons Act 1969, s. 1(2).

5   R.C.C.L. (op. cit.), para. 2.13 and Ch. 15.

6   [1986] A.C. 112.

7   Hewar v. Bryant [1970] 1 Q.B. 357, 369 per Lord Denning M.R.

8   See Eekelaar, "Gillick in the Divorce Court" (1986) 136 N.L.J. 184.

3.5   These matters will become still more relevant in our review of the wardship jurisdiction, in which the "welfare principle" has been applied to upset decisions by parents on single issues of upbringing,[9] to award care and control to people who are not parents,[10] to place a child in the care of a local authority,[11] and to attempt some control over children who are nearing majority.[12] We shall consider the scope and effect of the welfare principle further in Part VI, but for the moment we can assume that it will remain the governing criterion for most if not all of the decisions made in the jurisdictions under review here.

3.6   Even where it may be right in principle, determining what will best serve the interests of a child is fraught with difficulty. A great deal is already known about the growth and development of normal healthy children. Something is also known of the effects on that process of various types of upheaval or dislocation in the family and recently researchers have paid more specific attention to divorce.[13] Such evidence can provide us with valuable information and pointers towards the most desirable outcomes and how these might be achieved, but it can never provide the whole answer. First, the outcome considered "best" in the long term must depend upon social and cultural values rather than upon scientific judgments: it is for society to decide, for example, whether the child's present happiness should be put before his adult character and career, and to which aspects of adulthood it attaches most

---

9   Re D. [1976] Fam. 185.

10   J. v. C. [1970] A.C. 668.

11   Re C.B. [1981] 1 W.L.R. 379.

12   Re S.W. [1986] 1 F.L.R. 24.

13   For a review of the research literature, see Richards and Dyson, Separation, Divorce and the Development of Children: A Review (1982).

importance. Secondly, while "there are numerous competing theories of human behaviour ... no theory at all is considered widely capable of generating reliable predictions about the psychological and behavioural consequences of alternative dispositions for a particular child":[14] scientists, therefore, will find it just as difficult as judges to know how to achieve the best possible outcome in a particular case. Thirdly, the conclusions drawn from theory or empirical observation may differ so widely that their usefulness in terms of legal policy is difficult to determine: a common understanding of the importance of established attachments, for example, may lead one to argue that custody dispositions should be final and unconditional[15] and another that links with both sides of the family should be preserved and encouraged to the greatest extent possible.[16]

3.7   Nevertheless we believe it necessary to devise some yardsticks against which to judge whether proposed reforms in the law will indeed promote the welfare of the child as the first and paramount consideration. These yardsticks must be applicable, not only in the relatively small proportion of cases in which there is some dispute as to the person with whom the child is to live, but also in the much larger proportion where there is not.[17] Providing a criterion for the court's decisions is not, by itself, sufficient to secure that first, let alone paramount, consideration is given to the welfare of children who are involved in litigation. The whole

---

14   Mnookin, "Child Custody Adjudication: Judicial Functions in the Face of Indeterminacy" (1975) 39 L.C.P. 226, at p. 258.

15   Goldstein, Freud and Solnit, Beyond the Best Interests of the Child (1973), p. 37-39.

16   Wallerstein and Kelly, Surviving the Break-up: How Children and Parents cope with Divorce (1980), p. 310.

17   See para. 4.1 below.

process of legal intervention, including the role of the court itself, the orders which are available to it, the effect of those orders, and the method of deciding upon them, is equally important. We suggest that more precise objectives for the law of custody might be formulated thus:

(i) to separate, as far as it is possible, the issues relating to the children from those relating to any remedies sought between the parents or other adults involved, and to give priority to the former;

(ii) to recognise and maintain the beneficial relationships already established between the child, other children in the family and his parents or other adults who have been important to him and to encourage the continuation of these relationships to the maximum extent possible in the light of changed family circumstances;

(iii) to promote a secure and certain environment for the child while he is growing up, in which the confidence and security of the person who is bringing him up may be an important element;

(iv) to protect the child from the risk of harm to his physical or mental health, his proper physical, intellectual, social or emotional development, or his general well-being;

(v) to recognise, to the greatest possible extent, the child's own point of view, by ascertaining his wishes and feelings wherever practicable and giving due consideration to them, according to his age and understanding;

(vi)   to ensure that, where parental responsibility is divided or shared, the people concerned understand what legal responsibilities and powers they can and should exercise in relation to the child;

(vii)   to secure that, to the greatest extent possible, the legal allocation of powers and responsibilities reflects a state of affairs which is workable and sensible in everyday life.

3.8   We recognise that it may be impossible to achieve all of these objectives in every case. In particular, the reconciliation of aims (ii) and (iii) in the preceding paragraph can cause great difficulty; if it cannot be done, and they are evenly balanced, we suggest that priority should be given to (iii). Not only do we think this right in principle, once it has been determined where the child will have his home; we also believe that it is easier to predict what will promote the child's security in that home, which should not be put at risk for more speculative long-term aims. We nevertheless hope that the law can be so framed as to encourage rather than to impede the achievement of both objectives. We would also be grateful for comments on and suggested additions to the objectives we have put forward.

PART IV

THE ALLOCATION OF CUSTODY BETWEEN PARENTS

4.1   By far the most common occasion on which the custody of children arises between parents is on divorce.   Orders made in such proceedings represent some 80% of the total.[1]   The number of cases in which the issue arises, however, is greater than those in which an application or order is made, because before a decree can be made absolute the arrangements for the children must always be considered.[2] Thirty years ago only some 20,000 children were involved in divorce.[3]   In 1984 there were 144,501 divorces and 58% of these involved one or more children under the age of 16: in total 148,600 children.[4]   However, the number of divorces per year has remained broadly constant since 1980[5] while the child population has fallen,[6] so that the absolute numbers of

---

1   In 1985 approximately 90,000 custody orders were made in the High Court and county courts, 87,000 of which were made under the Matrimonial Causes Act 1973: see Lord Chancellor's Department statistics set out in the Supplement to this paper (Priest and Whybrow, Custody Law in Practice in the Divorce and Domestic Courts (1986)). In magistrates' courts 17,890 custody and access orders were made in guardianship and matrimonial proceedings in 1984: Home Office Statistical Bulletin 24/85, Table 2.

2   M.C.A. 1973, s. 41; see para. 4.4 et seq. below.

3   Royal Commission on Marriage and Divorce 1951-1955 (1956) Cmd. 9678, Chairman: Lord Morton of Henryton (the "Morton Report"), para. 360

4   O.P.C.S. Monitor FM2 85/1, Tables 1, 5b and 7.   (These figures include 755 annulments of marriage.)

5   Although there has been an increase in 1985 due to the reduction of the time bar on petitioning, ibid., Table 1.

6   O.P.C.S. Monitor FM2 84/1, page 2; Population Trends 43 (1986), Table 9, points to a levelling off of the decline in 1984 and the beginning of an upturn but the latter may be largely attributable to changes in the law, the effect of which is probably temporary.

children involved have also fallen.[7] Nevertheless it has been forecast that, if present rates of divorce and fertility are maintained, one in 22 children will experience their parents' divorce by the age of five, and one in five by the age of sixteen; and that one in three marriages will eventually end in divorce.[8] There are, therefore, a considerable number of children who are involved in some rearrangement of parental responsibility as a result of divorce and the largest proportion of these are (according to recent figures) between the ages of five and ten.[9]

4.2   Numbers alone might appear to justify concern for the fate of these children.   However, a system designed for the exceptional circumstances in which divorce used to arise is not necessarily appropriate once it becomes such a widespread experience.   It is important to emphasise here that the proportion of cases in which there is a contested hearing between the parties is very low, of the order of 6%.[10] This still represents a large number of children,[11] and the criteria employed by the courts in determining their future are likely to affect the

---

7   O.P.C.S. Monitor FM 2 85/1, Table 7.

8   Haskey, "Children of Divorcing Couples" (1983) Population Trends 31, pp. 20, 25 and "The Proportion of Marriages Ending in Divorce" (1982) Population Trends 27, p. 4.

9   In 1984 38% of children under 16 whose parents divorced were aged 5-10, 32% were aged 11-15 and 30% were 0-4: O.P.C.S. Monitor, FM2 85/1, Table 8.

10   See Maidment, Child Custody and Divorce (1984), pp. 61-62 and the sources therein.

11   Using the figure of 6%, approximately 9,000 children would have been subject to contested custody proceedings during their parents' divorce in 1985, which approaches twice the number of children committed to care in civil proceedings per annum (Children in Care in England and Wales (1983), Table A3).

decisions made by the parties themselves in other cases.[12] They will be considered further in Part VI. The usual question on divorce, however, as in other cases of parental separation, is how best the law can provide for those children whose future is not in dispute.

4.3   There are two aspects of the law to consider. The first is the role of the court and the second, the nature of the orders which the court should make.   These are closely related.   If it were thought that the court should not, in general, intervene in private family arrangements then it might also be thought that it was not necessary for the court to make orders relating to the child save where there is an issue to resolve, and that the orders available should reflect this minimalist approach.   A more interventionist policy, however, might require the court both to initiate action and to make orders governing every aspect of the child's life.

A. The role of the court

4.4   Proceedings for divorce, nullity and judicial separation are unique in requiring the parties to submit to the court for approval the arrangements to be made for all children of the family[13] under sixteen and some of those who are older: those under eighteen who are receiving education or being trained for a trade, profession or vocation, whether or not they are also employed, and those of any age whom the court has directed should be included because there are special circumstances (for example a mental or physical handicap) which make it desirable in their own interests.[14]   At present, the petitioner is required to file a separate written statement setting out the arrangements proposed for the children

---

12   See Mnookin, "Bargaining in the Shadow of the Law: The Case of Divorce" [1979] C.L.P. 65.

13   As defined by M.C.A.1973, s. 52(1); see para. 2.13.

14   Ibid., s. 41(1) and (5).

in the event of a decree being granted.[15]   Under the usual procedure, these are discussed with the judge at a private appointment after the decree nisi has been pronounced.   The judge must then declare that arrangements have been made for the welfare of each child and are either satisfactory or the best that can be devised in the circumstances, or that it is impracticable for the parties to make any arrangements.[16] "Welfare" includes not only custody and education, but also financial provision;[17] however, the court may sometimes be able to approve the arrangements even though these matters have not yet been resolved.[18] Alternatively, the court may declare that there are special circumstances making it desirable that the decree should be made absolute without delay even though such a declaration cannot yet be made.[19] Without a declaration, a decree of divorce or nullity cannot be made absolute.   In judicial separation cases, the declaration must be made before the decree.[20] If a decree is made or made absolute in the absence of a declaration, it is void; however if the declaration was made by mistake and, for example,

---

15   Matrimonial Causes Rules 1977, r. 8(2) and Appendix 1, Form 4. See further Rayden on Divorce 14th ed. (1983), p. 585 et seq.

16   M.C.A. 1973, s. 41(1)(b).

17   Ibid., s. 41(6).

18   As to the financial arrangements not being settled: Cook v. Cook [1978] 1 W.L.R. 994; Hughes v. Hughes [1984] F.L.R. 70 and Yeend v. Yeend [1984] F.L.R. 937.   A declaration may be granted pending resolution of a custody contest: A. v. A. [1979] 1 W.L.R. 533.

19   M.C.A. 1973, s. 41(1)(c).   If so, either or both parties must undertake to bring the future of the children before the court within a specified time, s. 41(2).

20   Ibid., s. 41(1).

not all the relevant children were named, or if undertakings given have not been observed, the decree cannot subsequently be challenged.[21]

4.5   This requirement arose from a recommendation of the Royal Commission on Marriage and Divorce which reported in 1956.[22]   The Commission thought it essential that everything possible should be done to mitigate the effect upon children of the disruption of family life.[23]   They referred to a "wealth of testimony" as to the effects on children of the breakdown of normal family relationships, where there was always the risk of a failure to meet fully the child's need for security and affection, which could result in emotional disturbance and anti-social behaviour.[24] The evidence they received suggested that there could be no guarantee that parents would always make the best arrangements for their children, particularly at a time when their own feelings were disturbed by the divorce.[25]   A court confronted by an unopposed application for custody would, in most cases, have little justification in refusing, yet the parents' apparent agreement might reflect a bargain between themselves rather than a desire to safeguard the child's interests.[26]   On the other hand, parents were usually the best judges of their children's welfare and the

---

21   Ibid., s. 41(3); Scott v. Scott (1977) 121 S.J. 391; Healey v. Healey [1984] Fam. 111.   Void was preferred to voidable, see Report on Financial Provision in Matrimonial Proceedings (1969) Law Com. No. 25, paras. 45-46, and for following conflicting case authority, see Rayden on Divorce (op. cit. at n. 15), p. 1100.

22   See n. 3 above.

23   Para. 362.

24   Para. 361.

25   Para. 366(iii).

26   Para. 366(ii).

arrangements made would always be limited by what was available.[27] Hence the Commission decided that a procedure was needed which would, first, ensure that parents themselves gave full consideration to the question of their children's welfare, even to the extent that they might decide not to pursue the divorce, and, secondly, enable the control of the court over the welfare of the children to be made more effective.[28] The Denning Committee before them had recommended that the divorce petitions be accompanied by a statement of the arrangements for the child.[29] Having being embodied in the Matrimonial Causes Rules 1947, this proved ineffective because the matters in question were not in issue before the court and the court had no means of enforcing compliance.[30] The Royal Commission therefore recommended that approval of the arrangements for the children be made a condition precedent to obtaining a divorce.[31] The possibilities of supervision or committal to local authority care in exceptional cases were also an essential part of the scheme,[32] which was first enacted in the Matrimonial Proceedings (Children) Act 1958.[33] The procedure for consideration and approval of arrangements now appears, largely unaltered, in section 41 of the Matrimonial Causes Act 1973.

---

27   Para. 371.

28   Para. 372.

29   Final Report of the Committee on Procedure in Matrimonial Causes (1947), Cmd. 7024.   See Murch, Justice and Welfare in Divorce (1979), Ch. 12.

30   See the Morton Report (op. cit. at n. 3), para. 379.

31   Para. 373.

32   Paras. 395 and 396.

33   Sections 5 and 6.

4.6   The original aims of section 41 could, therefore, be said to be:-

     (i)   to discourage or prevent divorce;

     (ii)   to ensure, by encouragement or court order if necessary, that parents who do divorce make the best arrangements they can for their children; and

     (iii)   to identify cases of particular concern where protective measures may be needed.

4.7   The operation of this provision has been the subject of research and criticism.[34] Although we cannot reproduce the details here, we will inevitably draw on this very valuable work in setting out what we believe to be the main arguments for and against the procedure.

---

34   Hall, Arrangements for the Care and Upbringing of Children (Section 33 of the Matrimonial Causes Act 1965) (1968) Law Commission Working Paper No. 15; Elston, Fuller and Murch, "Judicial Hearings of Undefended Divorce Petitions" (1975) 38 M.L.R. 609; Maidment, "A Study in Child Custody" (1976) 6 Fam. Law 195, 236; Eekelaar and Clive with Clarke and Raikes, Custody After Divorce (1977) Family Law Studies No. 1, Centre for Socio-Legal Studies, Wolfson College, Oxford; Eekelaar, "Children in Divorce: Some Further Data" [1982] O.J.L.S. 63; Dodds, "Children and Divorce" [1983] J.S.W.L. 228; Davis, MacLeod and Murch "Undefended Divorce: Should Section 41 of the Matrimonial Causes Act 1973 be Repealed?" (1983) 46 M.L.R. 121; Seale, Children in Divorce (1984) Central Research Unit, Scottish Office; see also the Australian Institute of Family Studies, Survey of Practices: Section 63, Family Law Act 1975 (1983). For further discussion of section 41 see Maidment, (op. cit. at n. 10), Chs. 3 and 6 and "The Matrimonial Causes Act, s. 41 and the Children of Divorce: Theoretical and Empirical Considerations" in State, Law and the Family Critical Perspectives ed. by Freeman (1984); Eekelaar, Family Law and Social Policy 2nd ed. (1984), Ch. 4 and Freeman, The Rights and Wrongs of Children (1983), Ch. 6.

Section 41 arguments

4.8   The arguments which can be advanced in favour of the system recommended by the Royal Commission are as follows:

(a)   The fundamental justification is the special risk of harm to all children whose parents divorce.[35] It is generally thought best for children to be brought up by their own united parents in a stable and secure environment.[36] A process which brings that state of affairs to an end inevitably carries a risk that the child's best interests will not be served, and in many cases there is a possibility of more serious harm.   At the very least, there is evidence that many children are surprised and shocked by their parents' separation, having themselves been happy despite the unhappiness of their parents, and some will persist for years in the hope that the family will be reunited.[37] These risks in themselves are sufficient to justify special measures in an attempt to minimise them.[38]

---

35   For reviews of the literature, see Richards and Dyson, Separation, Divorce and the Development of Children: A Review (1982) and Maidment (op. cit. at n. 10), Ch. 6.

36   See the Morton Report (op. cit. at n.3), para. 361; and in the words of the trial judge in a recent contested case: "all the court can do is to find what is second best because the proper situation and the only satisfactory situation is that those who bring children into the world should both help, together to look after them", quoted by Oliver L.J. in B. v. B. [1985] F.L.R. 166, 172.   See also Goldstein, Freud and Solnit, Beyond the Best Interests of the Child (1973), pp. 37-38.

37   Wallerstein and Kelly, Surviving the Break Up: How Children and Parents Cope with Divorce (1980); Mitchell, Children in the Middle (1985) and Walczak with Burns, Divorce: The Child's Point of View (1984).

38   See the conclusion of Davis, MacLeod and Murch (op. cit. at n. 34), pp. 142-3.

(b)   The procedure therefore ensures that the arrangements made by the parents are subject to some outside scrutiny, so as to identify those cases in which the parents' arrangements could be improved.[39] The whole process has been enhanced by the introduction of the special procedure in divorce,[40] which has reduced the formality in the hearings and made communication between parents and judges easier.[41] This has been coupled in many courts with an increased use of court welfare officers who can investigate, mediate and assist in the identification of difficult cases.[42]

(c)   Once those cases have been identified, the parties can be encouraged or obliged to make more suitable arrangements,[43] for otherwise they cannot be divorced. It is, for example, usual practice for courts to refuse to approve the arrangements where the parties are still living under the same roof and this will encourage them to resolve ancillary matters as quickly as possible, and with the housing needs of their children clearly in mind.[44]

---

39   See the Morton Report (op. cit. at n. 3), paras. 370 and 379; Davis, MacLeod and Murch (op. cit. at n. 34), pp. 137-9 and 145; see also Richards, "Behind the Best Interests of the Child: An Examination of the Arguments of Goldstein, Freud and Solnit concerning Custody and Access at Divorce" [1986] J.S.W.L. 77.

40   Matrimonial Causes Rules 1977 rr. 33 and 48; now in fact the usual procedure.

41   Murch (op. cit. at n. 29), Ch. 13; Davis, MacLeod and Murch (op. cit. at n. 34), pp. 133-136 and Dodds (op. cit. at n. 34), p. 231.

42   See Eekelaar ((1982) op. cit. at n. 34), and Davis, MacLeod and Murch (op. cit. at n. 34), p. 138-9.

43   Davis, MacLeod and Murch (op. cit. at n. 34), pp. 137-9.

44   Eekelaar and Clive (op. cit. at n. 34), para. 4.4.

(d) The section also provides a valuable opportunity to identify those children who are suffering such harm that the intervention of a local authority or welfare officer is needed.[45] The fact that in matrimonial proceedings about 500 children are committed to the care of local authorities and about 3000 put under their supervision annually indicates that section 41 plays a role in identifying and protecting such children.[46]

(e) Even if compulsory measures of protection are not required, the procedure provides a valuable means of help to parents who are having difficulty with their children or with making arrangements for them, by putting them in touch with the appropriate social services and other agencies.[47]

(f) The procedure can also be used to mediate between the parties. Where there are disputes, the requirement to appear in court can give the judge the opportunity to suggest solutions and to assist in reaching agreement. A judge may be able to achieve in a very

---

45 But see Davis, MacLeod and Murch (op. cit. at n. 34), p. 138-9, Dodds (op. cit. at n. 34), p. 237.

46 In 1982-1983 there were 440 committals to care under M.C.A. 1973, s. 43(1). Such committals form 9% of all committals to care by civil courts (excluding interim orders), 6% of all court committals (excluding remand and interim orders) and 1.3% of all admissions to care each year (Children in Care in England and Wales, (1983), Table A3. A similar return has been found since 1971, but between 1966 (50 orders) and 1971 there was a substantial increase. D.H.S.S. statistics show that in 1982-3 2,680 children were made subject to the supervision of English local authorities under section 44(1) of the 1973 Act and that the total number of children subject to such orders in that financial year was 14,877. The statistics are discussed further in the Supplement to this paper (op. cit. at n. 1).

47 Davis, MacLeod and Murch (op. cit. at n. 34), p. 139-40 and Eekelaar ((1982) op. cit. at n. 34).

short time what might take a skilled social worker several weeks.[48]
Even if the parties are agreed on the basic issue of where the child
should live, the appointment provides an invaluable opportunity to
establish desirable patterns of access and to promote co-operation
between the parents in the future. The court may be able to secure
joint custody and other orders for which the parties had not thought
to ask. In some courts, procedures have been devised very much
with these aims in mind, using the section far more positively than
had been originally intended.

(g) If the law insists that the first and paramount consideration be the
welfare of the child, it cannot sit back and let this be decided by the
parents. They are likely to be pre-occupied with their own
concerns at a time of severe emotional stress and often great
practical upheaval. Parents should at least be reminded of their
responsibilities towards their children.[49] This reminder also serves
to demonstrate the concern of the whole community that the well-
being of children should receive special consideration.[50] There is
evidence that divorcing parents understand this concern and
welcome rather than resent it.[51]

(h) Such a reminder is in fact a means of enhancing rather than
undermining the responsibility of parents. The procedure stops
short of requiring an independent investigation in every case, but

---

48 Davis, MacLeod and Murch (op. cit. at n. 34), p. 146.

49 See the Morton Report (op. cit. at n.3), para. 376 and Davis,
MacLeod and Murch (op. cit. at n. 34), pp. 138 and 146.

50 As with maintenance agreements see Hyman v. Hyman [1929] A.C.
601 and Sutton v. Sutton [1984] 1 Ch. 184, 196: the court must
consider the issue on behalf of the community at large.

51 Davis, MacLeod and Murch (op. cit. at n. 34), pp. 135-6 and 138.

informs the parents that they are expected to think of their children as well as themselves. The arrangements which they devise can be expected to be better in consequence.

(i) Finally, if this reminder causes the parents to reconsider their decision to divorce, this can only be of benefit to them, their children and the community as a whole.[52]

4.9 The following points can be made in opposition to each of the arguments in favour of the present system:

(a) There is no conclusive evidence to substantiate the premise that divorce is more harmful to children than many other events which may befall them.[53] Much of the earlier research indicating adverse effects upon the development and behaviour of children from "broken homes" failed to distinguish the different circumstances in which these arose.[54] It is also possible that the effects were caused as much by conflicts within the home as by the separation when it occurred.[55] Differing social expectations must now be taken into account, as the experience of divorce in the 1950s will have been very different from that in the 1980s.[56] There are also families in which divorce must be positively beneficial for the adults

---

52 Morton Report (op. cit. at n. 3), paras. 53-4 and 371.

53 Davis, MacLeod and Murch (op. cit. at n. 34), pp. 142-143.

54 Maidment (op. cit. at n. 10), pp. 161-176 and Richards and Dyson (op. cit. at n. 35), especially pp. 30-2.

55 Rutter, Maternal Deprivation Reassessed 2nd ed. (1981), for example, p. 131.

56 Richards and Dyson (op. cit. at n. 35), p. 10-11.

and children alike, for example, in cases of violence.[57]   Thus although there are undoubtedly children who suffer deeply, not only in the short term but also for a long time thereafter, it is impossible to say that these constitute such a large proportion of those who now undergo divorce as to justify special measures for their protection.

(b)   There is little reason to believe that the current procedures are effective in identifying those cases in which the parents' arrangements could be improved.[58]   This would require a full investigation of all the circumstances in every case.   The Royal Commission considered, but rejected, a proposal that the court should always have available an independent report upon the proposed home and surrounding circumstances.[59]   The information which is currently available to the court is very limited.[60]   The statement of arrangements itself is a standard form which seeks to elicit only basic facts about the children and very brief details of custody, access and maintenance arrangements.[61]   In some cases, perhaps inevitably, the questions are wrongly, carelessly or

---

57   See also Maidment (op. cit. at n. 10), p. 171 and the sources therein and Mitchell (op. cit. at n. 37), Ch. 5; but see Richards (op. cit. at n. 39), esp. at p. 89.

58   Davis, MacLeod and Murch (op. cit. at n. 34), pp. 137-9, and Dodds (op. cit. at n. 34), p. 236.

59   Morton Report (op. cit. at n. 3), para. 377.

60   Although in Dodds' survey 76% of divorce court judges felt that they receive all the information they want on which to make a decision (op. cit. at n. 34), p. 232.

61   Matrimonial Causes Rules 1977 Appendix 1 Form 4.   Some courts require further information even at this early stage: Davis, MacLeod and Murch (op. cit. at n. 34), p. 128.

evasively answered.[62]   Further the statement is usually filed by the petitioner only,[63] irrespective of whether he or she has actual custody of the children, and is completed at an early stage in the proceedings often before proper thought can be given to the matters in question.[64]   Only the petitioner is specifically required to attend the appointment.[65]   Although both parties are sent notice of the time and date and in some courts respondents are encouraged to attend, overall only a minority do so.[66]   Thus the judge is often only able to ask questions of one of the parties.   To supplement the information given the court does have power to call for a welfare report or for further information,[67] but this appears to be done in only 10% of cases,[68] although there is a wide variation in practice

---

62   Dodds, p. 230; Davis, MacLeod and Murch, p. 137; Hall, pp. 27-30, 37-38; Eekelaar (1982), pp. 70-1; Seale, Ch. 2 for the position in Scotland: all op. cit. at n. 34.

63   The respondent has the option of filing a statement, Matrimonial Causes Rules 1977, r. 50.

64   The statement of arrangements must accompany the petition (ibid.), r. 8(2).

65   Form D84.

66   Dodds (op. cit. at n.34) found that both parties attended in 28% of cases, although in the court which asked both to attend, 55% did so, p. 230. Davis, MacLeod and Murch (op. cit. at n. 34) found a dual attendance rate of 21%.

67   Matrimonial Causes Rules 1977, rr. 92(7) and 95.   Davis, MacLeod and Murch (ibid.) found that 3 out of 7 courts referred the names of the parties to the probation and/or social services, as part of the checking mechanism, p. 128-9.

68   Eekelaar and Clive (op. cit. at n. 34), paras. 4.4-4.6.   They concluded that "courts take their protection role seriously".

as to the number of welfare reports,[69] the circumstances in which they are made and the purposes for which they are sought.[70] The general impression is that reports are only obtained in unusual cases, perhaps, where the child has some medical problem or where there are difficulties, for example, with access.[71] In some courts it is usual for a welfare officer to be present or available but in others this is rarely, if ever, the case.[72] Further the judge may be hampered by the lack of time.[73] On average most appointments last around five minutes[74] and that is barely time for anything other than a perfunctory examination to take place.[75] Hence it has been said that the greatest weakness of the procedure is that it can give the impression of superficiality.[76] The changes introduced under the "special procedure" have not necessarily been sufficient to correct this.

---

69 Eekelaar and Clive (ibid.) found welfare reports in 8.2% of cases, frequency in the courts in their survey ranging from 18.4% to 3.1% ibid, para. 4.6 and Table 31. Davis, MacLeod and Murch and Dodds (op. cit. at n. 34, pp. 129 and 233, respectively) found welfare reports in an average of 5% of cases.

70 Eekelaar and Clive (ibid.), para. 4.7; Maidment (op. cit. at n. 10), pp. 73-78; James and Wilson, "Reports for the Court: The Work of the Divorce Court Welfare Officer" [1984] J.S.W.L. 89 and Wilkinson, Children and Divorce (1981) for detailed discussion of the work of divorce court welfare officers.

71 Dodds (op. cit. at n. 34), p. 234.

72 Davis, MacLeod and Murch (op. cit. at n. 34), p. 133.

73 In one survey the average listing per half day was 22.5 appointments: Davis, MacLeod and Murch (ibid.), p. 123-4.

74 Ibid. and Dodds (op. cit. at n. 34), p. 229, although the judges he interviewed did not see time as a problem.

75 Dodds (ibid.), pp. 229-30.

76 Hall (op. cit. at n. 34), p. 38.

(c)   Even if it is clear that the arrangements are less than satisfactory,
        the extent to which the judge can seek to improve them is strictly
        limited. As the Royal Commission itself observed, "the alternative
        to leaving the child in the charge of the parent would be to try to
        find a suitable relative or friend who is willing to undertake the care
        of the child or, failing that, that the local authority should receive
        the child into care; and it is obvious that conditions would have to
        be really bad before one of these courses could be justified".[77]
        Where the parents are agreed between themselves, the court cannot
        do much to oblige them to change their minds, nor is it likely to be
        in the child's best interests to do so. Hence researchers have
        concluded that the practical power of the court to produce different
        outcomes from those proposed is very small.[78] The evidence is
        clear that in the vast majority of cases the court sanctions the
        existing arrangements and very rarely is there any change in the
        child's residence as a result of the court proceedings.[79] Moreover,

---

77   Morton Report (op. cit. at n. 3), para. 371.

78   Eekelaar and Clive (op. cit. at n. 34), paras. 13.29-13.30; Hall (op.
      cit. at n. 34), Part 9; Maidment (op. cit. at n. 10), Ch. 3.

79   In uncontested cases in Eekelaar and Clive's study the child's
      residence differed from what it was at the time of the petition in
      2% of cases. In most of those the court sanctioned a change which
      had occurred before the final order (op. cit. at n. 34), para. 5.3. Of
      the 6% of contested cases, in only 2 (out of 39) did the court itself
      cause a change in the child's residence, although a welfare report
      was ordered in 53% of those cases and 62% of them were adjourned.
      Of the 2 cases of change, the one was made without a welfare
      report, the other was contrary to the officer's recommendation
      (ibid.), Ch. 6. Similar results were found by Maidment in a smaller
      study (op. cit. at n. 34). A higher degree of intervention was found
      by Eekelaar in his follow-up study of cases which had been referred
      to welfare officers: 23% involved court-ordered change in residence
      (7 out of 31 cases in which custody was contested at the hearing
      ((1982) op. cit. at n. 34), p.76). The data were thought to be more
      reliable although the cases are 'difficult' (ibid.), pp. 64 and 78. See
      also Maidment (op. cit. at n. 10), pp. 61-68.

once the arrangements have been approved there is no practicable means of ensuring that they are observed.[80] It is always open to the parties to depart from them, whether or not the circumstances change, and it is not easy to understand why they should not do so. Supervision may play a part in encouraging and improving the approved arrangements but it can only be made available in a small minority of cases where there is a particular problem to be resolved.[81]

(d) There is also little reason to believe that the procedure is either necessary or effective to protect the few children who are at special risk.[82] Committals to care in matrimonial proceedings are still a small proportion of all committals and a tiny proportion of the children whose parents divorce.[83] Any increase may well be accounted for by the increased availability of divorce to all sections of society. Many of the children so committed are already in the care of the local authority and most others will be known to the authorities in one way or another.[84] If they are not, it is probably a matter of chance whether they are identified by means of the

---

80 Hall (op. cit. at n. 34), pp. 40-41.

81 The number of supervision orders per annum is a matter of some doubt: see n. 46.

82 See para. 4.9(b) above and n. 58 in particular. Eekelaar and Clive comment "if the proper solution lies in committing the child to the care of a local welfare authority, it is arguable that the jurisdiction to do this already exists under the child welfare law ..." (op. cit. at n. 34), para. 13.25.

83 See n. 46.

84 See n. 67. See also the Supplement to this paper (op. cit. at n. 1).

current procedure.[85] In any event, these children are most unlikely to be suffering special harm as a result of the divorce itself, but rather because of underlying social or personal problems within the home.

(e) If families need to be put in touch with social and other services, there are several less elaborate and more effective means of doing so.[86] Information and addresses could be distributed, in busier courts officers of the local authority and D.H.S.S. could attend, and all parents could be offered an interview with a court welfare officer if desired. These could be a much more effective use of scarce resources than the investigation of every case, particularly as this can only be done properly by using more of the court welfare officers' time, which may be better spent in mediation and investigation in contested cases than in pursuing further inquiries into families where no obvious difficulties have arisen.[87]

(f) The functions of mediating between parties who are in dispute and of promoting co-operation in the future are indeed of crucial importance. It may be argued, however, that they are incompatible with the functions of a judge.[88] The process of mediation requires both time and sensitivity if the agreement reached is to be genuine and the parties are not to feel that they have been "rail-roaded" into

---

85   A matter of "guesswork and instinct", in the view of one judge quoted by Dodds (op. cit. at n. 34), p. 236.

86   See the suggestions of Eekelaar and Clive (op. cit. at n. 34), paras. 13.26-27 and Davis, MacLeod and Murch (op. cit. at n. 34), pp. 142-46.

87   See n. 42.

88   See Murch (op. cit. at n. 29), Ch. 13.

solutions which they cannot accept or put into operation.[89]   If
matters are in dispute it may be inconsistent with judicial
impartiality for the judge to express a view in an attempt to achieve
a resolution without a full hearing.[90]   The parties are bound to feel
that the matter has been pre-judged.   Furthermore, if the judge
tries to promote a particular policy or view of the best
arrangements, for example with regard to joint custody or the level
of access, this could be thought incompatible with the requirement
that each case be judged on its own individual merits in the light of
all the circumstances.[91]   There is even a risk (albeit not seen to
have materialised) that particular "hobby horses" will be ridden
without outside scrutiny or a real opportunity to challenge.[92]
Essentially, therefore, these functions are more suitable for skilled
welfare officers or social workers and should not be expected of
judges whose main task is to adjudicate upon disputes.   There is
evidence that, while some judges take a very positive and
constructive view, others would find difficulty in reconciling such an
approach with their more usual judicial functions.[93]

---

89   See Davis and Bader, "In-Court Mediation: The Consumer View"
     (1985) 15 Fam. Law 42, 82.

90   Murch (op. cit. at n. 29), p. 216.

91   Hence the Report of the Matrimonial Causes Procedure Committee
     (1985) Chairman: The Honourable Mrs. Justice Booth (The "Booth
     Report"), para. 4.132, rejected the suggestion that there be a
     presumption in favour of joint custody.

92   Murch (op. cit. at n. 29), p. 214.

93   Davis, MacLeod and Murch (op. cit. at n. 34), pp. 133-36.

(g) It is not clear that without the procedure parents would not act responsibly and make perfectly satisfactory arrangements for themselves. The Royal Commission accepted that "in the great majority of cases parents are the best judges of their children's welfare", so that where they are agreed upon the arrangements, "very strong evidence indeed would be required to justify setting aside their proposals."[94] The present procedure is not able to discover that evidence or to devise suitable alternatives in all but a tiny minority of cases. Furthermore, although leaving children entirely to the mercy of their parents may put them at risk of becoming pawns in the divorce proceedings, it is equally arguable that making arrangements for the children a procedural requirement of the divorce will put them similarly, if not more, at risk of the parents' proposing an arrangement simply to achieve their ends without particular regard to the interests of the children.[95] In any event, the law may be expecting too much. If the aim is to achieve arrangements which the judge thinks "satisfactory" in as many cases as possible, this is to impose upon divorcing parents a standard which may not be attained by many who are happily married.[96] It is all too easy for the courts to adopt a hypercritical attitude towards families simply because they appear in court. There is also doubt about the meaning of the current statutory targets. If the court certifies that the arrangements are the "best that can be devised in the circumstances", is this better or worse than

---

94 Morton Report (op. cit. at n. 3), para. 371, and see Mnookin, "Child Custody Adjudication: Judicial Functions in the Face of Indeterminacy" (1975) 39 L.C.P. 226, particularly pp. 264-8.

95 See Mnookin (op. cit. at n. 12).

96 And it is not the policy of the law that a child may be removed from his parents simply because he would be better off elsewhere: Review of Child Care Law ("R.C.C.L.") 1985, para. 15.10.

"satisfactory"? The section clearly regards this as second best, but that is not necessarily how it will appear to the parties. And how does either relate to the court's general duty to regard the child's welfare as the first and paramount consideration?

(h) The two main aims of the Royal Commission were themselves contradictory. On the one hand they wished to foster parental responsibility yet on the other to make the control of the court more effective. The result is an unhappy compromise in which the parents think that the court settles the arrangements and the court thinks that the parents do. Above all, however, it is wrong to single out parents who divorce as necessarily more irresponsible than others, just as it may be wrong to single out divorce itself as a greater occasion for concern than many other events causing distress or upheaval, such as the death or serious illness of a parent, separations arising in other circumstances, or the remarriage of a single parent, in none of which events are special measures taken.[97]

(i) The law has long recognised that there is little point in preserving the empty legal shell of a marriage and that once the relationship has irretrievably broken down the marriage should be dissolved "in a way that is just to all concerned, including the children as well as the spouses, and which causes them the minimum of embarrassment and humiliation".[98] This objective of good divorce law is just as valid today as when it was first postulated in 1966 and is just as applicable to the interests of the children involved as it is to their parents. Section 41 has clearly failed in its attempt to discourage divorce, and it has never been the policy of the law to make the

---

97   See the discussion in Maidment (op. cit. at n. 10), pp. 161-176.

98   The Field of Choice (1966) Law Com. No. 6, Cmnd. 3123, para. 17.

104

availability of divorce depend upon the presence or interests of the children.[99] Moreover, the relief of divorce may be most needed in precisely those cases in which satisfactory arrangements are most difficult to devise, because of the desperate situation of the family concerned; in those cases the existence of a procedure which assumes that the interests of children are always best served by the maintenance of the marital unit may deny them the very protection to which they are or should be entitled.

4.10   To sum up, the evidence suggests that the procedure has not been successful in any of its declared aims.   It certainly has not noticeably discouraged or prevented divorce, nor has it demonstrated any clear ability to secure better arrangements for the children of divorcing parents than the parents themselves would have devised.   It may have identified cases of concern that would not have been picked up by some other agency, but such cases are very rare.   Davis, Murch and MacLeod also concluded that as a means of offering help with personal or social problems or to mediate in disputes section 41 could be more effective.[100] Its most discernible virtue appears to be symbolic and incidental.[101] Given these findings, the case for some reform of section 41 would appear unassailable, but the direction in which it should go depends upon the balance of the arguments presented above.

---

99   Time Restrictions on Presentation of Divorce and Nullity Petitions (1982) Law Com. No. 116, paras. 2.34-2.35 and Working Paper No. 76, paras. 84-87.

100   Op. cit. at n. 34, p. 145.

101   Indirect benefits have been found in a study of the Australian equivalent, which also found that merely getting both parents together to discuss whatever problems exist between them in the courtroom setting can produce a speedy resolution of the issue: Australian Institute of Family Studies, Survey of Practices: Section 63 Family Law Act 1975 (1983), p. 18.

The options for reform

4.11   There would appear to be four broad options for reform:-

    (i)   to abolish the requirement altogether;

    (ii)   to improve the procedure while leaving the substance intact;

    (iii)   to strengthen both the substance and the procedure; and

    (iv)   to modify the substance so as to reflect more modest aims.

(i) Abolition

4.12   In principle, section 41 could probably be abolished.[102] The premises upon which it is based can no longer be substantiated and, to the extent that the procedure is superficial or ineffective, it may bring the law into disrepute. Abolition could, however, create the impression that the law no longer puts value on protecting the interests of children and we certainly would not wish to be thought of as encouraging parents to be irresponsible or not to consider the interests of their children when they divorce. It is an important function of the law to provide a model of behaviour which is generally believed to be desirable. This gives people an indication of what is expected of them and a framework in which they can negotiate between themselves.[103] Thus even a provision which has only symbolic usefulness may be of some value.[104] The procedure may

---

102   Davis, MacLeod and Murch (op. cit. at n. 34), pp. 143-5.

103   Mnookin (op. cit. at n. 12); Richards, "Post-Divorce Arrangements for Children: A Psychological Perspective" [1982] J.S.W.L. 133.

104   Davis, MacLeod and Murch (op. cit. at n. 34), pp. 141-2 and Dodds (op. cit. at n. 34), p. 237.

also give much needed protection to a few specially vulnerable children. The Booth Committee have expressed the view that section 41 should not be repealed unless something is put in its place.[105]   On balance, this is also our view.

(ii)   Improving the procedure

4.13   The Booth Committee have made several proposals for improving the procedure.   The statement of arrangements should contain much fuller information about the present and proposed arrangements, together with a statement of the claims made by the applicant in respect of the children.[106]   The respondent should be encouraged either to file the statement jointly with the applicant or to send in his own, particularly if he wishes to claim custody or access.[107]   In all cases where there are children to whom the section applies, an initial hearing before a registrar should be fixed at which, if the decree is granted, it should be possible for the court to satisfy himself as to the arrangements proposed.[108]   Thus the arrangements for children would be considered in much more detail and at an earlier stage in the proceedings than at the moment.   These proposals would meet some of the criticisms listed above, but they might compound others.   It would certainly be helpful if the same procedure could be adopted throughout the country.   It might also be useful if the court could do more to put parents in touch with whatever support services, conciliation, mediation, and social services, are available in the area.[109]   Improving upon the indirect effects of the court's duty would

---

105   Op. cit. at n. 91, para. 2.24.

106   Ibid., paras. 4.35 and 4.37.

107   Ibid., paras. 4.37 and 4.51.

108   Ibid., paras. 4.75 and 4.69.

109   Eekelaar and Clive (op. cit. at n. 34), paras. 13.26-27.

appear a more effective use of the resources available than strengthening its investigative functions.

(iii) Strengthening the substance

4.14 The provision could be replaced by some continental style bar to divorce if a divorce will substantially prejudice the interests of the children.[110] Such proposals have, however, always been rejected in the past because the effect of this on the children could be more harmful than divorce itself and we do not propose to consider them further here.[111] Alternatively, it might be possible to strengthen section 41 by giving the court powers of investigation and continuing control over the child's upbringing similar to those exercised by the court in wardship proceedings. This would be extremely expensive in resources and, we think, unjustifiable given the number of cases which can be identified as giving cause for concern and the limited scope which the court has for proposing alternative arrangements.

(iv) A more modest alternative?

4.15 At the other end of the spectrum the provision could be replaced by a mere injunction in the rules for parents to consider the interests of their children, perhaps by stating the proposed arrangements to the court as part of their petition. This, however, was unsuccessfully tried in 1947 and we accept that such aspirations need the support of some positive duty in the court. This duty could be to identify those children who require special protection, on similar grounds to those justifying the intervention of a local authority in care proceedings. This would, however, require as much, if not more, investigation and assessment than takes place at present, while carrying the unwarranted

---

110 In France, Germany and Belgium it is a bar to divorce if the dissolution of the marriage would prejudicially affect the children.

111 See n. 99.

implication that all children whose parents divorce are at such grave risk of harm. A more practicable solution could be to replace section 41 with a provision similar to that in section 8 of the Domestic Proceedings and Magistrates' Courts Act 1978, whereby the court's duty is to decide whether there are circumstances requiring an order to be made. At present the magistrates' court decides whether to make an order on the basis of the child's best interests. Thus the court would only need to examine whether there is a _prima facie_ case for an order and would not have to express a view as to how satisfactory a solution could be achieved. One merit of this approach is that it emphasises that the court need not make any order at all unless the circumstances require it, and we discuss this issue further below.[112] At the same time the formal scrutiny of the arrangements could provide a valuable opportunity to direct services towards those families and children who required them. In asserting the community's interest in the welfare of children, it would also hope to influence the approach of the parents themselves but without denying them the relief which may be as beneficial to the children as to them.

4.16   Hence our provisional view is that section 41 could be brought into line with section 8(1) of the 1978 Act. Although there is evidence that that section cannot effectively be applied under the present procedures available in magistrates' domestic courts, there is no reason to suppose that it could not be combined with improved procedures in the divorce courts along the lines proposed by the Booth Committee. We doubt, however, whether there is any longer any need to apply the procedure to children who have reached 16. For many school-leavers, it is a matter of chance whether they are employed, unemployed or on a training programme at the time of the hearing and it is certainly not obvious why the last should be singled out as in special need of attention.

---

112   Paras. 4.17-4.20 below.

In practice, the court is only likely to intervene in the most exceptional cases, as the extent of parental power over children who are old enough to make their own decisions is now extremely limited.[113] For the rare, perhaps handicapped, adult child who might at present be included as a special case, it is difficult to see how the court can help, given the lack of any power to make orders relating to custody or care, for financial matters can be and are dealt with independently of the duty in section 41.

B. The need for any order at all

4.17   The question here is whether it is necessary or desirable for the court to make an order in every case.   There are some cases at present in which no order is made, but usually, it seems, because there is a pre-existing magistrates' court order or the child is not the child of both parties.[114]   Otherwise, and sometimes even then, it is usually assumed that some order should be made.[115]

4.18   In the past, custody orders were an important feature of divorce proceedings simply because the father was sole guardian of a legitimate child and the mother could only acquire parental powers and responsibilities by court order or deed of separation.[116]   As mothers were the preferred custodians in so many cases, orders may have become the normal practice, even where they were strictly unnecessary.   This tendency has continued, although married parents now have equal rights

---

113   Hall v. Hall (1946) 175 L.T. 355.

114   See Eekelaar and Clive (op. cit. at n. 34), paras. 5.11-5.19.

115   See the Supplement to this paper (op. cit. at n. 1) and, for example, Laxton v. Laxton and Eaglan [1966] 1 W.L.R. 1079, a contested case.   Davies L.J. said that the court should make an order, although the decision could be postponed here for three months.

116   See Working Paper No. 91, Part II and Maidment (op. cit. at n. 10), Ch. 5.

and authority over their children.   The question now arises as to whether it should continue to be the normal practice to interfere in the status of the parties simply because they are separated or divorced.[117]

4.19   There are several arguments in favour of the usual practice:

(a)   As the court has a duty to oversee the arrangements made in the interests of the children, it should ratify those arrangements by means of court orders wherever possible; this makes it far more likely that the arrangements will be observed and, to some extent, preserves the court's ability to oversee them in the future, for example when applications are made for variation or revocation.

(b)   A regime of court orders is necessary in order to provide security and confidence for the children and the parent with whom they are living.[118]   The proportion of relatively amicable divorces may have increased, now that they are much more common and founded upon the irretrievable breakdown of the marriage rather than the commission of a matrimonial offence.   Nevertheless, divorce is almost always a time of great disruption and emotional upheaval and it is understandably comforting to have the child's situation determined, clarified and protected by court order.   There is still acrimony between the parties in a large number of cases and the proportion in which there is or has been violence is remarkably

---

117   See Cretney, Principles of Family Law 4th ed. (1984), p. 402 and Maidment (op. cit. at n. 10), particularly Ch. 12.

118   See, for example, Goldstein, Freud and Solnit, Beyond the Best Interests of the Child (1973).

high.[119]   The children usually live with their mother[120] and she may be continually fearful that they will be taken away by the father or that he will seek to interfere in their upbringing in other ways.   The children's interests cannot be well served if the person with whom they are living and who is carrying the main burden of responsibility for them finds that her ability to go on doing so is threatened in such a way.

(c)   Court orders are also necessary in order to provide a structure which clarifies the respective positions of both parents.[121]   Where the parents no longer live together, the children will normally have to make their home with one or the other; cases in which their time can be more evenly divided than it is at present may increase but will remain a minority for the foreseeable future.[122]   The parties need to know where that home will be and how the children's time is to be divided.   They also need to know what will be the children's relationship with the other parent, whether and when he will be able to see them and what other parental responsibilities he will be able to exercise.   Leaving matters unclear is likely to increase rather than decrease animosity and litigation.

(d)   For as long as court orders remain the normal practice, these advantages can be secured without the risk of increasing acrimony.

---

119   See Cretney (op. cit. at n. 117), p. 234 n. 7 and the sources therein cited.

120   In approximately 90% of cases: see the Supplement (op. cit. at n. 1).

121   See, for example, Richards (op. cit. at n. 103), p. 148 and (op. cit. at n. 39), p. 90.

122   See, for example, Maidment (op. cit. at n. 10), p. 261.

If, however, it became normal practice for orders to be made only when expressly sought and there was special reason to do so, an application could be seen as a hostile step even between parents who were relatively amicable.[123] Even if the parent with whom the children were living had good reason for seeking an order, she might be deterred by this extra hurdle. It would also place her in a less favourable position when bargaining for other features of the divorce settlement as a whole, in that she might be inclined to concede property and financial support (even on behalf of the children) in order to achieve a clear and secure right to custody.[124] If so, the children's own interests could be damaged as much as those of their parent.

(e) Finally, it is not only necessary that the children and parties should know their respective legal positions. Others, in particular housing authorities, schools and education authorities, doctors and other health service professionals, as well as the D.H.S.S., may need to know with whom the child will be living and what, if any, responsibility remains with the other parent.[125]

4.20 There are, however, counter-arguments favouring a different approach:

---

123 For a discussion of the consequences of introducing statutory preferences for certain results in child custody adjudications see Schulmann and Pitt, "Second Thoughts on Joint Custody: Analysis of Legislation and Its Impact for Women and Children" (1982) 12 Golden Gate University Law Review 539, drawn on by Weitzman, The Divorce Revolution (1985), p. 245.

124 Ibid. and Mnookin (op. cit. at n. 12).

125 See the Supplement (op. cit. at n. 1).

(a)   We have already argued that the court's existing duty to approve the arrangements should be replaced with a less stringent requirement.[126]   The court's ability to ensure that the approved arrangements are kept is in any event limited.[127]   The parents should not feel inhibited in changing their arrangements if it is necessary or desirable to do so.   It is no more practicable or sensible to require them to go back to court every time they decide, for example, that a child will see more of his other parent than it is when the child changes schools or the custodial parent moves house. Some parents probably understand this, but others may feel obliged to continue the arrangements ordered by the court even if they are united in wishing to change them.

(b)   While it is certainly necessary in some cases to provide security for the children and the parent with whom they are living, in others this may have positively harmful effects.   Where a child has a good relationship with both parents, the law should interfere with this as little as possible.   Orders allocating custody and access can have the effect of alienating a child from one or other of his parents, and the evidence is that this is rarely what the child himself wants.[128] It is always difficult for the parent with whom the child is no longer living to continue to behave like a parent.[129]   This will be exacerbated if the orders made encourage the parent with whom the child is living to "stand upon her rights".   Nor should the law give

---

126   Para. 4.16 above.

127   See para. 4.9(c) above.

128   See the sources at n. 37.

129   See para. 4.32 below.

the impression that custody of children is one of the spoils to be won or lost in the war of divorce.[130]

(c) The present orders available do not clarify the position.[131] Although they could probably be improved, it is doubtful whether they could ever be made sufficiently precise to allow parents to know exactly where they stand upon every point about which they might disagree. If so, it might be better to interfere as little as possible, and use court orders simply to decide those matters which are in dispute or to ratify the broad outlines of what has been arranged. Anything else could be a recipe for more bitterness and disagreement.

(d) In most cases, orders of some sort will still be desirable. There is therefore no reason to believe that the need to make application for one will be seen as a hostile step or place the parent who wishes for an order in a less favourable bargaining position. If this were to be the case, however, it would undoubtedly be a serious objection to any change in the existing law or practice.

(e) The courts' practice in allocating responsibility between parents should be governed by the needs of the children and not by administrative convenience. In particular, it is inappropriate for the courts to be used as a means of determining questions such as eligibility for social security benefits or local authority housing when otherwise there would be no need for a particular order to be made.

---

130   Parkinson, "Joint Custody" (1981) 7 O.P.T. 10, 13.

131   See paras. 2.34-2.50 above and 4.23 et seq below.

4.21   In our view, these arguments favour a flexible approach in which the court does not assume that it is necessary to make comprehensive orders for the re-allocation of every aspect of parental responsibility but equally is ready to make whatever orders will be most helpful in the particular cases before it.   However desirable it may be to interfere as little as possible in parental relationships, the security and comfort of the child may depend upon the security and confidence of the parent with whom the child is living and who is carrying the day-to-day burden of responsibility, and should be given priority.[132]   There remains, however, the question of what orders should be available and whether there should be any statutory preference between them.

C. The orders available

4.22   We have already seen that only two types of order are commonly made by divorce courts at present.   These are:

(i)   sole custody to one or other parent (the mother in 77 per cent of cases and the father in 9 per cent of cases) usually with access to the other;

(ii)   custody to mother and father jointly (13 per cent of cases) usually with care and control to one and access to the other.[133]

The so-called "split order" in which custody was given to one parent and care and control to the other is now rarely made and has, for the reasons

---

132   See for example, M. v. J. (1977) 3 F.L.R. 19, 26 per Balcombe J.

133   See paras. 2.34-2.50 above and, for the Statistics, the Supplement to this paper (op. cit. at n. 1).

explained earlier, been judicially described as undesirable.[134] Under the Domestic Proceedings and Magistrates' Courts Act 1978 and the Guardianship of Minors Act 1971, therefore, the court cannot separate legal from actual custody; nor can it make a joint custody order as such, although it may allow the party deprived of legal custody to retain some or all of the rights it contains, apart from actual custody, sharing them with the custodial parent.[135] In addition to this discrepancy, each of the orders available has its difficulties and disadvantages.

Sole custody

4.23   The main difficulty with a sole custody order under the Matrimonial Causes Act 1973 is that its legal effect is no longer clear. It may appear to grant[136] the custodial parent control over almost every aspect of the child's life, with the specific exceptions of changing his surname and taking him abroad.[137] However since the decision in Dipper v. Dipper[138] it is not clear whether:

(a)   the custodial parent may exercise responsibility over each aspect of the child's upbringing (with those two exceptions) unless the other parent applies to the court;[139] or

---

134   Dipper v. Dipper [1981] Fam. 31, 45 per Ormrod L.J. and Caffell v. Caffell [1984] F.L.R. 169, 171 per Ormrod L.J., but see Jane v. Jane (1983) 4 F.L.R. 712 and para. 2.42 above.

135   See paras. 2.45-2.47 above.

136   Although the divorce court's order is in terms of retaining custody: see Forms D61 and D53 which are used by the divorce registries. A similar form appears in Rayden on Divorce (op. cit. at n. 15), p. 4140, c.f. Magistrates' Courts (Matrimonial Proceedings) Rules 1980 Schedule, Form 13 "legal custody .... be given".

137   See paras. 2.51 and 2.58 above.

138   [1981] Fam. 31.

139   Guardianship Act, s. 1(1); Cf. Dipper v. Dipper (ibid.) and Jane v. Jane (1983) 4 F.L.R. 712.

(b)   she may exercise responsibility over each aspect unless the other
        parent has signified disapproval, in which case <u>she</u> must apply to the
        court;[140] and

(c)   if (b) is the case, it applies only to major matters of upbringing;   if
        so, what those major matters are;[141] and whether (a) applies to the
        rest;   and

(d)   in any event, she must consult the non-custodial parent before
        taking major decisions, so that he may object or apply to the court
        as the case may be.[142]

4.24   Were it not for the observations of the Court of Appeal in
<u>Dipper</u> v. <u>Dipper</u> the answer to these questions would be governed by
whether or not the independent power of action conferred upon each
parent by section 1(1) of the Guardianship Act 1973 had been made
subject to the power of veto contained in section 85(3) of the Children
Act 1975.[143]   It is doubtful whether this effect was ever intended,
although it may well have been accomplished.

---

140   Children Act 1975, s. 85(3).

141   In <u>Dipper</u> Ormrod L.J. spoke of "the education of the children, or
       their religious upbringing or any other major matter in their lives",
       (<u>op. cit.</u> at n. 138), p. 45.

142   In <u>Dipper</u> Cumming Bruce L.J. said that both parents are "entitled"
       to know and be consulted about the future education of the children
       and any other major matters" (<u>ibid.</u>), p. 48.   Ormrod L.J. said that
       "neither parent has any pre-emptive right over the other" (<u>ibid.</u>), p.
       45.

143   See para. 2.2 above.

4.25   Following _Dipper_ v. _Dipper_ the effect of a sole custody order
is almost certainly to confer upon the custodial parent a power of
independent action with regard to day-to-day matters or care and
control,[144] but it may be that the non-custodial parent has a veto power
over other "more strategic matters". Yet if it were thought appropriate
for each of united parents to be able to take decisions about the child
without reference to the other, it must in some cases be even more
appropriate for a sole parent to do so.   The number of marital
breakdowns in which one spouse has behaved in such a way as to call in
question his fitness to play a large part in bringing up the children should
not be underestimated.[145]   Alternatively, he may be uninterested,
irresponsible, or so hostile that he would be likely to exercise a veto
power in a way which made life extremely difficult for the child and the
custodial parent.   They cannot be expected to go back to court every
time a decision has to be taken about matters in dispute.   As we have
already said,[146] where preserving the stability and security of the child's
home conflicts with preserving every aspect of the legal relationship with
his other parent, the former should prevail.

4.26   Even in these cases, however, it may be appropriate for the
non-custodial parent to maintain a voice in some matters, whether by way
of veto or by way of a requirement of consent.   The latter approach is
already taken with respect to changes of surname and taking the child out
of the country.   These may be the most important, in that each can have
a particularly serious effect upon the relationship between the child and
his other parent.   The courts appear more prepared to approve a move

---

144   In _Caffell_ v. _Caffell_ [1984] F.L.R. 169, 171, Waller L.J. said that
       "the mother who has the care and control and is mainly responsible
       for the daily upbringing of the two children should have custody".

145   See n. 119.

146   Para. 3.8 above.

abroad,[147] which can seriously disrupt contact between parent and child, than to sanction a change of surname,[148] which need have no such effect, although it will be open to the child to adopt whatever surname he likes when he comes of age.[149] There are obvious advantages in spelling out in the order itself those matters over which the non-custodial parent is to retain some control and the method of that control. Indeed, this is one advantage of the provision for sharing specified rights under the 1978 and 1971 Acts.

Access

4.27   Whatever the arguments in favour of giving the custodial parent independent power of action, there are also arguments in favour of preserving the relationship between the child and the non-custodial parent.[150] The usual means of doing this is an access order, which will be granted unless it is clearly contrary to the child's interests. Numerous studies,[151] however, testify to the problems which access can cause, for both of the parents and for the child, and it is known that there are far more disputes, and far greater difficulties of enforcement, in access than in custody itself. The studies also reveal a tendency for access to

---

147   Poel v. Poel [1970] 1 W.L.R. 1469 and Chamberlain v. de la Mare (1982) 4 F.L.R. 434.

148   W. v. A. (Child: Surname) [1981] Fam. 14.

149   He may change his name informally below that age but at 16 may enrol a deed poll evidencing his change of name, Enrolment of Deeds (Change of Name) Regulations 1983 S.I. 680.

150   Wallerstein and Kelly (op. cit. at n. 37); Leupnitz, Child Custody: A Study of Families After Divorce (1982); see further Maidment (op. cit. at n. 10), Ch. 10 and the sources therein.

151   See, most recently, Maidment (ibid.); Richards (op. cit. at n's. 39 and 103); Eekelaar ((1984)op. cit. at n. 34), pp. 70-72; Wilkinson (op. cit. at n. 70), Ch. 4; Mitchell (op. cit. at n. 37), Ch. 6.

diminish, often quite quickly after the divorce, and in a substantial proportion of cases it ceases altogether within two or three years of the separation.[152]

4.28   In earlier studies, more attention was given to the problems which access might bring to the custodial parent and to the child.[153] It can revive unhappy memories of a marriage she would like to forget. Both parents may be tempted to renew hostilities through their children.[154] There may be resentment that the non-custodial parent is better-off, or is able to provide treats and gifts, while the custodial parent carries the day-to-day burdens alone.   Regular arrangements may cause inconvenience, while irregular arrangements or those which are not kept will cause disappointment and upset.   The custodial parent may see only the immediate unsettling effect on the child and find the more speculative long-term benefits difficult to appreciate.

4.29   From the child's point of view, there is no doubt that access can be unsettling and upsetting.[155] Children are often unaware of the

---

152   Maidment (ibid.), p. 238-9, referring to Maidment (op. cit. at n. 34), Eekelaar and Clive (op. cit. at n. 34), Murch (op. cit. at n. 34).   For experience elsewhere see Ahrons and Sorenson, "Father-Child Involvement" in Cseh-Szombathy et al (ed), The Aftermath of Divorce - Coping with Family Change, An Investigation in Eight Countries (1985).

153   Maidment (ibid.), p. 236 and sources therein cited;   see also Maidment, "Access Conditions in Custody Orders" (1975) 2 B.J. Law and Soc. 182, pp. 185-187.

154   It has been found that children under sole custody arrangements may be more prone than joint custody children to being used in parental power games, for example in the withholding of support and access: Grief, "Fathers, Children and Joint Custody" (1979) 49 American Journal of Orthopsychiatry 311.

155   See the sources at n. 37 and n. 151.

problems in their parents' marriage and feel let down or abandoned when one of them goes. Loyalty conflicts can easily arise, having adverse effects on the relationship with both parents. They may be subject to spoken or unspoken pressure from either parent and can eventually react by refusing to see the non-custodial parent at all. Hence it has been argued that children have such difficulty in maintaining positive relationships with both parents that "the non-custodial parent should have no legally enforceable right to visit the child, and the custodial parent should have the right to decide whether it is desirable for the child to have such visits."[156]

4.30   The more general view, however, is in accordance with that of Latey J. in M. v. M. (Child: Access):[157]

> ".... where the parents have separated and one has the care of the child, access by the other often results in some upset in the child. These upsets are usually minor and superficial. They are heavily outweighed by the long-term advantages to the child of keeping in touch with the parent concerned, so that they do not become strangers, so that the child later in life does not resent the deprivation and turn against the parent who the child thinks, rightly or wrongly, has deprived him, and so that the deprived parent loses interest in the child and therefore does not make the material and emotional contribution to the child's development which that parent by its companionship and otherwise would make."

Thus it will benefit the child to continue to have two parents; not to feel that one has abandoned or been denied to him; to know properly rather than to fantasise about the other parent; to learn to live in two different households and to cope with and enjoy two different sets of relations and

---

156   Goldstein, Freud and Solnit (op. cit. at n. 36), p. 38; c.f. Richards and Dyson (op. cit. at n. 35), p. 64 and Richards (op. cit. at n. 39).

157   [1973] 2 All E.R. 81, 88.

expectations: to enlarge rather than confine his experiences. Such evidence as there is supports the view that continued contact is associated with the best long-term outcomes for the child.[158]

4.31　　However convinced we may be of the benefits of continued contact, it is difficult to know how best the law can encourage it. The children who benefited from it might have done so whether or not there was a legally enforceable right to access, because of positive attitudes in both parents. Without such attitudes, the law is often powerless. If the custodial parent, or the children themselves, are implacably opposed, there is little the court can do unless a change of custody is a realistic alternative.[159] Perhaps more important, there is at present nothing the court can do to require the non-custodial parent to keep in touch. Despite these difficulties, we believe that the law should continue to recognise, in appropriate cases, the right of a non-custodial parent to continued contact with his child, if only to set standards for the whole family. We would welcome suggestions as to what further steps could be taken to persuade both parents of the merits of this.

4.32　　In part, this depends upon why so many non-custodial parents lose touch.[160] There are many reasons about which the law can do little. For example, some may be uninterested. Others may believe, wrongly, that if they do not see their children they will not have to pay maintenance or, conversely, that if they are not paying maintenance they are not entitled to access. Some are inhibited by the considerable

---

158　Richards and Dyson (op. cit. at n. 35), sources at n's. 150 and 151, Murch (op. cit. at n. 29); and Ahrons and Sorenson (op. cit. at n. 152).

159　See para. 2.57 above.

160　See particularly Richards (op. cit. at n. 103); Murch (op. cit. at n. 29), Ch. 4.

practical difficulties involved, particularly if they have moved to another part of the country or cannot arrange for staying access or are in financial difficulties. Above all, perhaps, the exercise of access itself can be difficult and painful for the non-custodial parent. It is hard to maintain a parent-like relationship with a child who is only seen from time to time, the more so the shorter or less frequent the access is or if it cannot take place in the parent's own home. This can produce the unnatural "Father Christmas" syndrome, in which the relationship does indeed depend upon treats and gifts. Paradoxically, therefore, the more the non-custodial parent cares about the child, the more painful access may become: the more, indeed, he may be tempted to believe that it is better for the child if he keeps away.

4.33   There may be two ways in which the law could make a greater contribution towards solving these problems. First, there is at present little or no guidance as to what constitutes "reasonable access". To devise guidelines would be a task of some difficulty, for there is a great diversity of professional opinion on the matter.[161] There is also a risk of interfering unnecessarily in arrangements which the family have made to their own satisfaction. However, there may be a tendency to assume that if access is not working well, it should be reduced,[162] whereas some of the factors mentioned earlier would point in the opposite direction. Provided that the parent with whom the child is not living is not tempted to carry on the marital battle by putting pressure on the child, they are

---

161   Cf. e.g. Richards and Dyson (op. cit. at n. 35), pp. 52-53 and Justice Report on Parental Rights and Duties and Custody Suits (1975), p. 54; in Norway, there is an express preference for visits once a week, one afternoon a week, every second weekend, two weeks in the summer holidays and during Christmas or Easter holidays, see Moxnes in Cseh-Szombathy (op. cit. at n. 152), p. 202.

162   See Richards (op. cit. at n. 39).

more likely to maintain a healthy parent child relationship the more they see of one another, and this could apply most strongly to younger children who have more difficulty in appreciating abstract relationships and retaining them during separation.[163]

4.34   Secondly, the law might do more to recognise the continued parental status of the parent during access, so that he does not feel inhibited in exercising the normal responsibilities of care and control. One means of doing this, which is becoming increasingly popular, is the joint custody order.

Joint Custody

4.35   A number of factors have contributed to the rise in popularity of joint custody orders in this country and elsewhere.   First, there has been an increasing recognition that the task of bringing up children is not the exclusive responsibility of one parent but a shared responsibility of them both.[164]   If this is the case in fact, then it should also be the case in law.

4.36   Secondly, for the reasons already given, it is widely thought that continued contact with both parents is the best way of promoting the children's welfare.   If so, joint custody may encourage the parent with

---

163 Which could explain why they seem to suffer more rather than less from a marital breakdown: see Wallerstein and Kelly (op. cit. at n. 37).

164 For a review, see Rapoport, Rapoport and Strelitz, Fathers, Mothers and Others (1977).

whom the children are no longer living to play a greater role.[165] It avoids the "public acknowledgement and notice that the role of the non-custodial parent is expected to be reduced".[166] At the very least, it should improve his position during access and perhaps his willingness to exercise access at all. It avoids the hurtful "winner takes all" impression which a sole custody order may give.[167]

4.37   Thirdly, the increase in divorce, its relative acceptability and the wider range of circumstances in which it may be granted have perhaps increased the number of cases in which there is the possibility of close co-operation between the parents following their divorce. These facts may also have contributed to the view that the "once and for all" disposition which was appropriate when divorce was a rare (and perhaps a shameful) event is no longer appropriate when it is the experience of so many children. They should be able to feel that their lives have been disrupted as little as possible by their parents' separation.

---

165 Caffell v. Caffell [1984] F.L.R. 169 and Hurst v. Hurst [1984] F.L.R. 867. Support for this proposition may be found in Wallerstein and Kelly (op. cit. at n. 37); Leupnitz (op. cit. at n. 150); Roman and Haddad, The Disposable Parent: The Case for Joint Custody (1978); see further Parkinson (op. cit. at n. 130), Maidment (op. cit. at n. 10) pp. 262-265, and Cseh-Szombathy (op. cit. at n. 152), pp. 175 and 214. As to the applicability of American research in this country see Richards and Dyson (op. cit. at n. 35), pp. 10-11.

166 Richards (op. cit. at n. 103), p. 148.

167 Some non-residential parents clearly value the joint custodial status, Leupnitz (op. cit. at n. 150) p. 40. Some custody disputes may be caused by the perceptions of divorcing parents: custody terms may have the potential to "discourage parental co-operation and increase the likelihood of conflict": Patrician, "Child Custody Terms: Potential Contributors to Custody Dissatisfaction and Conflict" (1984) Mediation Quarterly 41, 54. See also Chapman, "Custody" (1985) 1 N.Z. Law Bulletin 30.

4.38   This may have been further encouraged by the reduction in the relevance of matrimonial fault, both in the ground for divorce and in the allocation of custody in disputed cases.[168]   There is an understandable desire to treat each parent equitably, and in some cases perhaps to award joint custody as a "consolation prize" to the parent, usually the father, with whom the children will no longer be living.   In one study[169] it appeared that joint custody was more commonly awarded where custody had originally been contested.   Although this is probably less so today, it may be a tempting means of achieving a settlement, which in itself can be in the best interests of children who would otherwise suffer from the delay, uncertainty and bitterness engendered by a contest.

4.39   In England and Wales joint custody commonly means that legal responsibility for taking "strategic" decisions as to the child's upbringing is shared, while one parent has day-to-day care and control and the other has access.   The strict legal effect is to render section 85(3) of the Children Act 1975 undoubtedly applicable, so that over the matters not contained in "care and control" either party may act unless the other signifies disapproval.   Both parents are thus deprived of the totally independent power of action which they may previously have enjoyed under the Guardianship Act 1973, but the parent without care and control acquires both a decision-making power and a veto power which he would not otherwise have had.   Although such orders should usually be made only where there is a reasonable prospect of co-operation between the parties, courts do not always insist upon this[170] or upon the consent of

---

168   For example, Re K. [1977] Fam. 179.

169   Eekelaar and Clive (op. cit. at n. 34), para. 6.6;   Caffell v. Caffell [1984] F.L.R. 169 could be an example.

170   Jussa v. Jussa [1972] 1 W.L.R. 881, as interpreted by the Court of Appeal in Caffell and Hurst (op. cit. at n. 165).

both parents.[171]   Joint custody orders are not, however, desirable where there is a potential for conflict which could put the child at risk.[172]

4.40   Although these orders have gained in popularity in some parts of the country (largely in the south), in others (largely in the north) they are still quite rare.[173]   The attitudes and expectations of courts, legal practitioners and the parties themselves must play some part in this.   In any event, these orders clearly have disadvantages.   The main benefit appears to be purely symbolic, in recognising the continued parental status of the other parent.   But this is not a genuine sharing of parental responsibility, for all the major burdens of looking after and bringing up the child are still carried by the parent with whom the children are living. To the extent that it may encourage the other parent to interfere in day-to-day matters it is obviously undesirable.[174]   Lack of clarity about the division between "strategic" and "day-to-day" matters can only make this worse.

---

171   R. v. R. [1983] C.L.Y. 336.

172   Jane v. Jane (1983) 4 F.L.R. 712.

173   See the Supplement (op. cit. at n. 1).

174   Schulman and Pitt (op. cit. at n. 123); Wilkinson (ibid.), pp. 34-35; Brophy and Smart, Women-in-Law: Exploration in Law, Family and Sexuality (1985) Ch. 5.   Research seems to point to the promotion of co-operation rather than conflict through joint custody: Leupnitz (op. cit. at n. 150) p. 150; Maidment (op. cit. at n. 10), p. 261, 266, c.f. Weitzman (op. cit. at n. 123), p. 255-256.   Similarly disagreement exists as to relitigation rates following joint and sole custody orders: Ilfeld et al, "Does Joint Custody Work?   A First Look at Outcome Data of Relitigation" (1982) 139 American Journal of Psychiatry p. 62 c.f. Weitzman (ibid.).   However it seems clear that hostility at the time of separation and divorce need not rule out successful joint custody: Parkinson (op. cit. at n. 130), Goldzband, Consulting in Child Custody (1982), p. 35.

4.41   Furthermore, it is in many cases almost impossible to separate strategic decisions from the day-to-day responsibilities of care and control. If the parent with whom the children are no longer living is able to play an equal part in deciding where they shall go to school or to church, it is the parent with whom they live who will usually have to put this decision into practice, by taking the children there or insisting that they go. Even "strategic" responsibilities cannot in practice be exercised without also having care and control of the child.   There is thus a considerable danger that joint custody will become either "power without responsibility" or, what may be worse, responsibility without power.

4.42   Research indicates that the majority of joint custody orders result in the mother taking care and control where otherwise she would have obtained sole custody.[175] The traditional division of responsibility, in which the mother carries the day-to-day burden but the father is able to exercise some control over how this is done, may thus be perpetuated. Yet the more popular such orders become, the more difficult the mother may find it to resist one even when it is not so appropriate in her case.

4.43   Finally, there are still cases in which the needs of the child and the custodial parent to feel secure and free from even the unlikely threat of interference must be put before the symbolic advantages of joint custody, even if this also increases the risk of the child and the non-custodial parent losing touch with one another.

Shared custody
4.44   The objections to joint custody according to the model in England and Wales might not apply so strongly were care and control

---

175 See the Supplement (op. cit. at n. 1) and for California, Weitzman (op. cit. at n. 123), p. 253 and more generally Ahrons and Sorenson (op. cit. at n. 152).

itself to be shared or more evenly divided. In the United States of America, the reaction against divisive custody dispositions which give the non-custodial parent "little chance to serve as a true object for love, trust and identification since this role is based on being available on an uninterrupted day to day basis",[176] has been answered by a movement towards joint physical custody which aims to provide "that physical custody of the children somehow be shared in such a manner as to ensure frequent and continuing contact between the children and both parents".[177] There has been much research, albeit of limited general applicability, which points to the success of joint custody after divorce in providing for emotional continuity and a network of support for children.[178] Some States have therefore enacted a presumption in favour of joint custody, which includes joint physical custody, which can on occasions be applied irrespective of the wishes of the parents.[179]

4.45   We see the force of the arguments in favour of joint custody in the sense of sharing the benefits and burdens of being a parent.[180]

---

176   Goldstein, Freud and Solnit (op. cit. at n. 36), p. 38.

177   Goldzband (op. cit. at n. 174), p. 34.

178   See Johnston, "Shared Custody After Parental Separation" [1982] N.Z.L.J. 8; Ahrons, "The Continuing Co-Parental Relationship between Divorced Spouses" (1981) 51 American Journal of Orthopsychiatry 415; Leupnitz (op. cit. at n. 152) and Maidment (op. cit. at n. 10), Ch. 11.

179   E.g. California Civil Code §4600, 4600.5 and Weitzman (op. cit. at n. 123), Table C-7; under New Zealand law, joint custody means joint physical custody: Johnston (ibid.). Shared care and control is also relatively common in some Scandinavian countries: Moxnes (op. cit. at n. 152).

180   As one father said "it's a lot better to have 100 percent of the responsibility 50 percent of the time than 50 percent of the responsibility 100 percent of the time", quoted in Leupnitz (op. cit. at n. 150), p. 43.

However, although on occasion it may be difficult to distinguish from sole custody with liberal staying access,[181] it seems that shared care and control is most exceptional on this side of the Atlantic. There are strong doubts as to whether joint physical custody in the American sense is generally practicable. It particularly relies on the feasibility of joint child care to which society is not generally geared.[182] Also the imposition of joint custody in cases where one parent is reluctant may cause much stress and practical difficulty for the child and parents.[183] For some children the dividing of time between two homes may be against their best interests,[184] particularly if it involves switching between schools and friends. A child who moves between two families may not regard himself, or be regarded, as a full member of either. For his parents, running two homes may duplicate expenditure and add to their financial problems. It has thus been argued that it could lead to decreased maintenance for the mother, whose fixed costs nevertheless remain as high as if she had sole custody.[185] Finally, if the sharing does not turn out to be equal the order may be little different from joint custody in the English sense.

---

181 See Goldzband (op. cit. at n. 174), p. 35 and Steinman, "The Experience of Children in a Joint Custody Arrangement" (1981) 51 American Journal of Orthopsychiatry 403.

182 Brophy and Smart (op. cit. at n. 174); Roman and Haddad (op. cit. at n. 165).

183 Steinman (op. cit. at n. 181); Leupnitz (op. cit. at n. 150) and Goldzband (op. cit. at n. 174).

184 See, for example, R. v. R. (1986) The Times, 28 May 1986.

185 It is said that joint custody arrangements permit fathers to seek lower levels of child support. Hence an income-sharing rather than a cost-sharing scheme for calculating child support is advocated: Weitzman (op. cit. at n. 123), p. 361, 391-395.

4.46   In conclusion, most commentators have warned of the need to approach each custody decision case by case, and therefore that the case for a legal presumption in favour of joint custody has not been made out.[186] Further, research has not pointed out what marks an appropriate case for joint custody: conflicts between parents at the time of the divorce does not mean that joint custody is unworkable and the degree of co-operation between parents is not necessarily the same before and after a divorce.[187]

The options for reform

4.47   Some reform is clearly required, because of the uncertainties surrounding the existing law of custody under the Matrimonial Causes Act and the discrepancies between that Act and the other enactments. There appear to be three main options:-

(i)   to leave the courts a completely free choice;

(ii)   to provide for essentially the same orders as at present but to clarify their effects; and

(iii)   to attempt a new approach.

(i)   A free choice

4.48   The court in all jurisdictions might simply be given power to make such order relating to the parental powers and responsibilities as it sees fit.[188] This would retain both the generality and the flexibility

---

186   See, for example, Steinman (op. cit. at n. 81).

187   Ibid., Goldzband (op. cit. at n. 174), p. 36, quoting Benedek and Benedek, and Ahrons and Sorenson (op. cit. at n. 152), pp. 183-184; see also Richards (op. cit. at n. 39), pp. 87-90.

188   See Law Reform (Parent and Child) (Scotland) Act, s. 3(1). This is also the position in Maine.

hitherto achieved under the Matrimonial Causes Acts. Unfortunately, it would carry exactly the same risk of uncertainties arising as has happened under the present law. Furthermore, courts would in practice have to devise common forms of order, and it would be difficult for them to achieve both clarity and consistency in their effects.

(ii)   Clarifying the present orders

4.49   Under this model, the present doubts and inconsistencies would be removed, but the options would remain broadly those discussed above. Thus the court might order:

(a)   Sole custody

This would give the custodial parent power and responsibility over every aspect of the child's upbringing save any matter expressly dealt with in the order (such as taking the child abroad or changing his name). The other parent would always be able to apply to the court if he disagreed with any decision, and the order might specify matters of which the custodial parent had to keep him informed (such as changes of address or school).

(b)   Joint custody, with sole care and control

This would give one parent power and responsibility over the child's everyday life, but would give them both power and responsibility over certain long-term matters; it would be desirable for the law to clarify which matters fell into which category, and this might pose difficulties; it would also be desirable to spell out whether each retained an independent power of action or was subject to the other's veto on long-term matters; once again the order might specify matters on which each had to keep the other informed or on which consent or the leave of the court was required.

(c)   Joint custody, with shared care and control

This would be as above, but the child would divide his time between the two, either as agreed between them or as specified by the court (although if such specification were required, it is perhaps unlikely that the order would be appropriate). Alternatively, the court might make no order at all; however, in the aftermath of divorce, some couples may find terms such as "joint custody" reassuring.

(d) Access

Along with orders (a) or (b), but not (c), the court might also order that the child be permitted to see, visit or have such other contact as the court may specify with the parent with whom he is not living. The order could be phrased in this "child centred" rather than "parent centred" way. We invite views as to whether further guidance on what is "reasonable" should be given, either by the law or by the court in appropriate cases; the latter could be done by indicating whether day-time, overnight or staying visits were reasonable, or by suggesting a minimum or maximum within which the parties might seek to make their arrangements; it could, however, be difficult to do this without hearing more evidence than is at present usual in uncontested cases, so that the dangers of pre-judging might outweigh the advantages of setting a framework for the parties' own discussions.

4.50   There are many advantages in this approach. The old "split order" would not be revived, but the court would have a range of options to meet the many different circumstances which can arise. Terms which are now "well enough" understood, despite their technical uncertainties, could be retained and clarified. Legal and actual custody, as defined by the Children Act 1975, would, however, be replaced by the terms as described above. There would be no presumption as to which was most appropriate in any one case, and thus any pressure on the parent with whom the child is living for most of the time would be kept to a minimum. Spelling out the options in the legislation might, however, provide some incentive for those who do not currently consider alternatives to sole custody to do so. On the other hand, the disadvantages of "joint custody" would remain essentially untouched and confusion might be caused by giving slightly new meanings to current terms.

134

(iii) A possible alternative

4.51   It may be a mistake to see custody, care and control and access as differently-sized bundles of powers and responsibilities in a descending hierarchy of importance.   A parent who is exercising access, for whatever period of time, must have all the responsibility of someone with actual custody.[189]   If, for example, a child spends the weekend with his father on an access visit his father (and also the father's new wife if he has one) will have full responsibility for and power to decide what the child eats, when he goes to bed, whether and where he goes to church, what he does with his time, to summon medical attention in the event of an accident or illness, and so on.   The legal effect of the mother's disapproval of any of these things is uncertain and could only be resolved by returning to court.[190]   Obviously the range of powers and responsibilities will vary according to the period of time involved, but for so long as the child is with the parent that parent will have all the day-to-day care and control status that the parent with "custody" or "care and control" has when the child is with her.   Perhaps, therefore, the division of responsibility between parents with custody and care and control or access, respectively, is temporal rather than qualitative.

4.52   If this is right, the arrangement is more one of "time sharing" than an allocation of specific bundles of powers and responsibilities to one or other.   There is some support for this approach to parental responsibility in the views of Lords Fraser and Scarman in <u>Gillick</u> v. <u>West Norfolk Area Health Authority</u>,[191] to the effect that a parent's rights flow from his duty to protect the child and thus arise primarily from his

---

189   Children Act 1975, s. 87(1) and (2).

190   See para. 4.23 above.

191   [1986] A.C. 112, 170 <u>per</u> Lord Fraser, 184 and 185 <u>per</u> Lord Scarman.

physical custody, rather than parental status as such. The task of the court could therefore be to decide, in general terms, the allocation of the child's time between his parents, each of which should have care and control while he is with them.

4.53   There are several advantages in regarding post-divorce arrangements in this light:-

(a)   It would not be necessary to make invidious allocations of powers and responsibilities between parents. It need not be suggested that one parent is better or more fit than the other, simply that the child is able to spend more time with one or the other.

(b)   Implicitly, there may be some encouragement towards a more equal distribution of time and with it the day-to-day responsibility for the child. We believe that such arrangements should be encouraged where they are desired by both parents, although they should never be imposed upon the unwilling.

(c)   The upgrading of access should in any event reduce some of the difficulties faced by the parent who is exercising it.

(d)   Parental powers and responsibilities would be given substance by the fact of care and control. If we are to think in terms of parental responsibilities rather than parental rights, as we think we should,[192] and accept that such responsibilities are difficult to exercise properly in the absence of care and control, power and responsibility should go hand in hand and largely "run with the

---

192   See Illegitimacy (1982) Law Com. No. 118, para. 4.18 and Working Paper No. 91, para. 1.11.

child". This should be preferable to the current type of joint custody order in which one parent has physical care and control but the other has some ill-defined powers of intervention or decision.

(e)   Each parent would retain his parental status and with it his power of independent action, just as each has (or at least should have) during marriage.   In the event of a dispute, recourse could be made to the court, again just as it can by parents during their marriage.

4.54   However, there will always be some matters in respect of which this cannot provide the complete answer.   Questions which can arise independently of care and control are to some extent already dealt with by statute or rules of court:

(a)   Change of surname and leaving the country require consent or leave of the court, unless the court has directed otherwise.   It might be considered whether a consultation and veto power were not more sensible in each case, but these are matters which may be so important that positive consent is appropriate.

(b)   The requirement of agreement to adoption is unaffected by divorce or the reallocation of custody, although in certain circumstances it may be dispensed with.[193]   It may however be questioned whether the same should not also apply to the qualifications for custodianship.   Certainly the matter should be considered in the context of third party rights generally.[194]

---

193   Children Act 1975, ss. 12 and 14.

194   See paras. 5.20 - 5.26 and 5.35 below.

(c)   The policy of the Marriage Act 1949 seems to be to remove the power to consent to marriage from the non-custodial parent but to preserve it where the child's time is divided between the parents.[195] This matter could perhaps be dealt with in the court order rather than the statute, so as to preserve the parent's power in appropriate cases.

(d)   The parents' rights and duties in relation to state education are covered by the Education Acts, and are not expressly affected by a custody order,[196] although it seems that some education authorities are willing only to deal with the custodial parent unless there is a joint custody order. Once again, this matter need not be affected by a court order, unless dealt with expressly. Where private education is concerned, the power of the purse is usually sufficient to ensure that the other parent is consulted, but in appropriate cases this could be expressly provided for in the order.

4.55   In our view, the sensible method of dealing with each of those decisions which can arise irrespective of care and control is by individual express provision appropriate to the matter in question. This would leave each parent and third parties knowing exactly where they stood. It would also, on some if not all matters, allow the court's order to be tailored to meet the needs of the individual case.

---

195 See para. 2.52 above.

196 Although "parent" is defined in s. 114(1) Education Act 1944 as including a guardian and everybody who has the actual custody of the child the parents' duty to secure the child's education is not limited by the fact that the child is not living with the parent or is in the actual custody of someone else: Rennie v. Boardman (1914) 111 LT 713 and London School Board v. Jackson (1881) 7 QBD 502, and either parent may be liable, whether or not they are living together: Woodward v. Oldfield [1928] 1 KB 204 and Plunkett v. Alker [1954] 1 QB 420.

4.56   There may be no other matters which require to be dealt with in this way, but there are at least two possible candidates:

(a)   In some, but by no means all, cases it may be appropriate to require consent or permit a veto upon changing the child's religion.   In practice, however, it is particularly difficult to separate religious observance from care and control and if the dispute is sufficiently serious the matter will have to be decided by the court in any event.

(b)   It may, very occasionally, be appropriate to preserve the power to consent to serious medical treatment, perhaps in cases where the parent with care and control has religious objections to blood transfusions or operations.   It is less easy to see how a power of veto, over and above the usual power to refer disputed questions to court, could be beneficial, as the treatment should in any event be medically indicated in the best interests of the child.[197]

4.57   Under this model, therefore, the equality of parental powers conferred by the Guardianship Act 1973 would be preserved or, to the extent that it has been modified by the Children Act 1975, restored.   The normal order on divorce or separation would allocate only care and control as appropriate in the particular case.   Any restrictions, qualifications or conditions upon the exercise of parental responsibilities during care and control would be dealt with by statute or spelled out in the order.   We do not doubt that there will be cases where it will be appropriate for a parent to have care and control only for limited periods of time and on condition that he or she does not interfere, for example, with the child's established habits of religious observance or medical treatment or deliberately flout the other parent's wishes in respect of some particular matter.

---

197   Gillick v. West Norfolk and Wisbech Area Health Authority [1986] A.C. 112.

D. Conclusion

4.58   We provisionally favour the new approach outlined in the immediately preceding paragraphs. Although the discussion has hitherto concentrated largely on divorce, we see no reason why it should not be applied to all jurisdictions in which custody is currently allocated between parents. The reasons for encouraging parents to share as much of their responsibility as is possible following their separation apply just as, if not more, strongly to separations falling short of divorce.

4.59   Hence the final scheme could have the following main features:

(i)   Parents who were married to one another when the child was born or conceived would have equal parental powers and responsibilities and be able to act independently of one another at any time, unless and until otherwise provided.

(ii)   A court before which any of a list of matrimonial remedies was claimed would be under a duty to make such investigations of the arrangements made or proposed for the children of the parties under 16 as would enable the court to decide whether to make an order with respect to the parental powers and responsibilities, and if so which. Rules of court would make more detailed requirements in relation to each procedure.

(iii)   In any such proceedings, or on the application of the mother or father of a child, the court should have power:

(a)   to share care and control of the child between them for such periods or in such a manner (for example, between residential care and control and visiting care and control) or subject to such conditions as it sees fit;

(b)   further to specify the nature or times of visiting care and control, for example as day-time, over-night or holidays, as it sees fit;

(c)   to specify those matters over which the parent who for the time being has care and control is not to retain the independent power of action; the more common of these could be provided for in rules of court;

(d)   to resolve any particular question arising between the parents as to the exercise of their parental powers and responsibilities.

(iv)   It should be made clear that, except where provided for in any such order, the parents were to retain their parental status and powers of independent action.

(v)   It should also be made clear that, unless specifically prohibited by the court, the parties remain free to modify the arrangements by agreement between them, although such an agreement would not be enforced if the court were of the opinion that it would "not be for the benefit of the child to give effect to it."[198]

---

[198]   This is the wording currently adopted in relation to the enforcement of agreements between husband and wife in the Guardianship Act 1973, s. 1(2).

PART V

THE ALLOCATION OF CUSTODY AND ACCESS TO NON-PARENTS

5.1   In Part IV we were able to assume that parents should have unrestricted access to the courts for the purpose of seeking custody of or access to their children.   The issues were therefore confined to the role of the courts[1] and the orders which might be available to them.[2]   These issues also arise in relation to the award of custody or access to non-parents, but the prior question concerns the circumstances in which the courts should have power to make such awards, whether in the course of proceedings initiated by others or at the instance of the non-parent concerned.   By "non-parent" we mean anyone other than the child's natural or adoptive mother and father, such as step-parents, relatives, people who have taken a child into their family by private arrangement with the parents, foster parents with whom a child has been boarded-out by a local authority or voluntary organisation, or indeed anyone else who may have an interest in the child or be concerned for his welfare. Although these may seem useful categories in practice, they are not consistently employed by the law.   Indeed, it is difficult to discover any consistent principle now underlying the complexities of the law in this area.

A.   Who may be granted custody or access?

5.2   At present, there are three broad categories of people other than parents who may be granted custody of a child:

---

1   See paras. 4.4-4.16 above.

2   See paras. 4.22-4.57 above.

(i) spouses who have treated the child as a member of their family for the purpose of matrimonial proceedings between those spouses;[3]

(ii) people who are qualified to apply for custodianship[4] or for adoption;[5] and

(iii) people to whom the court wishes to grant custody in the course of matrimonial[6] or Guardianship of Minors Act[7] proceedings initiated by spouses or parents.

5.3   There are three, rather different, categories of people who may be awarded access:

(i) spouses who have treated the child as a member of their family may be granted access, not only in matrimonial proceedings between themselves,[8] but also if a custodianship order is made;[9]

(ii) grandparents may be granted access if a custody order is made in proceedings between spouses under the

---

3   M.C.A. 1973, ss. 42 and 52(1); D.P.M.C.A. 1978, ss. 8 and 88(1): see paras. 2.13-2.15 above.

4   C.A. 1975, s. 33(3): see paras. 2.24-2.27 above.

5   C.A. 1975, ss. 10 and 11 [Adoption Act 1976, ss. 14 and 15].

6   M.C.A. 1973 s. 42; D.P.M.C.A. 1978, s. 8(3): see paras. 2.18-2.19 above.

7   C.A. 1975, s. 37(3); G.M.A. 1971, ss. 10(1) and 11(a): see paras. 2.21-2.22 above.

8   M.C.A. 1973, s. 42; D.P.M.C.A. 1978, s. 8.

9   C.A. 1975, s. 34(1)(a) and (2).

Domestic Proceedings and Magistrates' Courts Act 1978[10] or between parents under the Guardianship of Minors Act 1971[11] or if the parent who is their child has died[12] or if a custodianship order is made;[13]

(iii) any person, if given leave to intervene, may be granted access to a child of the family in divorce or other proceedings under the Matrimonial Causes Act 1973.[14]

5.4 The reasons for each of these categories may readily be understood in the particular context in which they arose, but, taken as whole, they produce anomalies and inconsistencies[15] which it is difficult either to understand or to justify.

Spouses

5.5 By far the most common occasion upon which courts could grant custody or access to non-parents is in divorce or other matrimonial proceedings. In practice, of course, the great majority of the spouses involved will be step-parents. 32,048 of the 144,501 marriages dissolved

---

10 Section 14.

11 Section 14A(1).

12 Section 14A(2).

13 C.A. 1975, s. 34(1)(a).

14 See para. 2.18 above and Matrimonial Causes Rules 1977, r. 92(3). A guardian, step-parent, a person who has custody or control of the child under a court order or a local authority having care or supervision of the child by an order under the M.C.A. does not need leave to intervene.

15 See paras. 2.13-2.33 above.

in 1984 were second marriages for one or both parties.[16]   In one
sample,[17] 8.7% of the children involved in divorce were from a previous
relationship.   Second marriages in younger age-groups (where there are
perhaps more likely to be such children) carry a greater risk of breaking
down than do first marriages or second marriages of older couples.[18]   It
is not known how many of the "children of the family" involved in divorce
proceedings are not the child of either party to the marriage, but the
proportion is likely to be very small.

5.6   When their marriage breaks up, spouses who have treated a
child as a member of his family are themselves treated almost like
parents, with regard to custody, access, financial provision and the court's
duty to approve the arrangements made for the child.   The only
difference is that, in awarding financial provision, the court must take
into account whether, to what extent and on what basis the spouse
assumed financial responsibility for a child who was not his own, whether
he did so knowing that the child was not his, and the liability of anyone
else to maintain the child.[19]   Furthermore, any person in relation to
whom a child was treated as a child of the family may be granted access
or ordered to make financial provision if a custodianship order is made.[20]

---

16   O.P.C.S. Monitor FM2 85/1, Tables 1 and 2.

17   From our own survey of 6 courts' figures for 1985:   see the
      supplement to this Working Paper: Priest and Whybrow, Custody
      Law in Practice in the Divorce and Domestic Courts (1986).

18   Haskey, "Marital status before marriage and age at marriage: their
      influence on the chance of divorce" (1983) Population Trends 32, p.
      4.

19   M.C.A. 1973, s. 25(4) and D.P.M.C.A. 1978, s. 3(4).

20   C.A. 1975, s. 34(1)(a) and (b), s. 34(2).

Similarly, under the Inheritance (Provision for Family and Dependants) Act 1975, provision may be ordered out of the estate of a deceased person for anyone whom the deceased has treated as a child of the family in relation to any marriage to which he was a party.[21]

5.7   This state of affairs appears the natural evolution of the powers of divorce courts to provide for the welfare of all the children who might be affected by the break-up of a particular marriage.   Courts hearing divorce and other matrimonial causes were first given power to make orders relating to children who were not the legitimate, legitimated or adopted children of both parties to the marriage by the Matrimonial Proceedings (Children) Act 1958.[22]   The Morton Commission had recommended an extension to legitimate or illegitimate step-children who were living in the family when the home broke up, and also to "other children (excluding boarded-out children) who were living in the family with the spouses and maintained by one or both of them at the time when the home broke up."[23]   These children were just as much in need of the Commission's recommended procedure for investigating the arrangements for their welfare as were children of the marriage.   Once the court was given that task, it could scarcely be denied the power to make the orders necessary to secure what it believed to be the best available outcome.

5.8   The corollary, however, was the potential imposition of a liability to maintain, and there were clearly doubts about how far such a

---

21   Section 1(1)(d).

22   Section 1(1).

23   Royal Commission on Marriage and Divorce 1951-1955 (1956) Cmd. 9678, para. 393.

new departure should be taken.[24] In the 1958 Act, therefore, the court's powers were limited to children of one party who had been "accepted" by the other (i.e. to certain step-children).[25] Later case-law made it clear that although acceptance involved the co-operation of both parties, a man could not be said to have accepted a child whom he wrongly believed to be his own.[26]

5.9   In 1967, however, the matter was reconsidered by the Law Commission in the particular context of financial provision in matrimonial proceedings.[27] It was there pointed out that "To say that a man should not have to maintain a child unless he is related to the child by blood or adoption can be justified logically. But once one goes beyond that, there is no logical or just stopping place short of acceptance into the family. It makes no sense to couple that with a relationship by blood or adoption to the _other_ party to the marriage."[28] Responsibilities may have been

---

24   Illegitimate children of one of the parties to the marriage were excluded from the original Bill because it was thought that it would be necessary to amend the existing laws for maintenance if they were included (Hansard (H.C.) vol. 581, col. 1495). These children were eventually included by a clause inserted during the Standing Committee stage (Standing Committee C, 12th March 1958 (1957-8) vol. 11, col. 45 et seq.) after criticism of their exclusion during the debate of the Bill in the House of Commons.

25   Children who are not the children of either of the parties to the marriage were excluded because "it will not only give rise to difficulties as to responsibility for maintenance but to difficulties in connection with impending legislation to revise the whole of the powers of the magistrates' courts ..., in relation to separation and maintenance": Report of the Standing Committee (ibid.), col. 50. The matter is not, however, referred to in the Report of the Departmental Committee on Matrimonial Proceedings in Magistrates' Courts (1959), Cmnd. 638.

26   R. v. R. [1968] P. 414 and B. v. B. and F. [1969] P. 37.

27   Working Paper No. 9, Matrimonial and Related Proceedings. Financial Relief, paras. 165-173.

28   Ibid., para. 168.

assumed and relationships established whenever a child is treated as a member of the family, as for example when a step-parent assumes responsibility after the death of a parent, remarries and then the subsequent marriage breaks up: the children's needs for custody, access and financial provision will be just the same on the break-up of the second marriage as they were on the first.[29]

5.10   Hence, in 1969 the Commission recommended the present definition.[30]   It was agreed that the Morton Commission's suggested limitation to children who were currently living in the family (and, for those other than step-children, being maintained by one or both) could not be justified, as those who were not might be the most in need of the court's protection.   The key was how both spouses had behaved towards the child and one party's knowledge of the facts (although relevant to financial provision) should not affect the court's power to do what was best for the child: the cases had revealed that such a party might well be anxious to maintain contact with children whom he had regarded as his for so long.[31]   Children boarded out by a local authority or voluntary organisation should be excluded, as they were the responsibility of the child care agency.   Other foster children would be covered if they had indeed been treated as members of the family, and not, for example, as relatives coming to stay for school holidays while parents were abroad. However, orders made on divorce would not affect the rights and liabilities of natural parents,[32] whereas those relating to step-children

---

29   See the example at para. 169 (ibid).

30   Financial Provision in Matrimonial Proceedings (1969), Law Com. No. 25, para. 30.

31   Ibid., paras. 27-29; see B. v. B. and F. [1969] P. 37.

32   Ibid., para. 31.

would continue to bind a parent who was made a party to the proceedings.[33]

5.11   These proposals were enacted in what is now the Matrimonial Causes Act 1973,[34] and subsequently extended to matrimonial proceedings in magistrates' courts[35] (although it appears that orders made there will affect the rights of parents if they have been given an opportunity to be heard).[36]   Once it had been accepted that there could be financial liabilities towards children who were not one's own, a similar approach could be adopted towards family provision on death, but here it was thought that the obligation of the deceased should depend only on how he himself had behaved towards the child and not, as in divorce, upon what both spouses had done.[37]

5.12   By these steps, therefore, spouses who have treated a child as a member of their family have acquired almost the same status in legal proceedings as have parents. Their position is not, of course, identical, in that they have no automatic parental status and cannot initiate proceedings for custody or access alone, as can parents under section 9 of the Guardianship of Minors Act 1971. Further, if a parent does initiate such proceedings, a spouse who has treated the child as a child of his family cannot be granted access, although he could be granted legal custody by means of a "custodianship direction",[38] and he could be

---

33   See paras. 2.16 and 2.17 above.

34   Sections 42(5) and 52(1).

35   D.P.M.C.A. 1978, s. 88(1).

36   See para. 2.17 above.

37   Inheritance (Provision for Family and Dependants) Act 1975, s. 1(1)(d).

38   C.A. 1975, s. 37(3).

granted access if a parent were granted custody in proceedings between spouses under the Domestic Proceedings and Magistrates' Courts Act 1978 or if a third party became custodian.[39]

5.13   The provisions just discussed all operate when the spouses' relationship has in some way come to an end, by death, divorce or separation.   Before that, it may sometimes be possible to acquire parental status in relation to a child who is not one's own.   If the child has been named as a "child of the family" in previous divorce proceedings, usually between his parents, then any person may seek leave to intervene in the divorce suit to acquire custody and a step-parent may do so without leave.[40]   The law encourages step-parents to do this rather than to seek adoption,[41] but it appears that very few do so.[42]   Adoption is well understood and gives the step-parent and custodial parent (and often the non-custodial parent too) all they want, whereas returning to the divorce court to seek joint custody may seem a great deal of trouble for little gain.   We have already raised, in our Guardianship paper, the possibility of custodial parents appointing step-parents guardians to share their parental responsibilities in such circumstances.[43]

---

39   Section 8(2)(b).

40   See para. 2.18 above.

41   C.A. 1975, ss. 10(3) and 11(4): see para. 2.32 above.

42   Masson, Norbury and Chatterton, Mine, Yours or Ours? (1983), p. 85; Priest, "Step Parent Adoptions: What is the Law?" [1982] J.S.W.L. 285.

43   Working Paper No. 91 (1985), paras. 4.15-4.19.

5.14   However, if there have been no divorce proceedings in which the child was involved, the only way in which a step-parent or indeed any other person who has taken a child into his family can apply for custody (before his own marriage ends) is by qualifying for custodianship.[44]   He cannot apply for access at all.   Thus the step-parent of a child whose birth parents were not married to one another or whose other parent has died is in a less favourable position than the step-parent of a child whose parents are divorced.   On the other hand, if a quite different person is granted a custodianship order, a person in relation to whom the child was treated as a child of the family may not only apply for access but may also be ordered to make financial provision.[45]   Furthermore, any applicant who has to qualify for custodianship must have the child living with him at the time of the application,[46] whereas a person who may initiate or intervene in divorce proceedings need not.

Custodians

5.15   Custodianship was devised to meet two distinct needs.   The Houghton Committee on the Adoption of Children[47] was mainly concerned to provide an alternative to adoption by step-parents (which had by then become very common, especially after divorce)[48] or by

---

44   C.A. 1975, s. 33.

45   C.A. 1975, s. 34(1)(a) and (b);   s. 34(2).

46   C.A. 1975, s. 33(3).

47   Report of the Departmental Committee on the Adoption of Children (1972) Cmnd. 5107, Chairman (until November 1971):   Sir William Houghton (the "Houghton Committee").

48   Ibid., paras. 97 and 103 to 110.   See also Masson, Norbury and Chatterton, Mine, Yours or Ours? (1983), pp. 1 to 3.

relatives such as grandparents.[49]   Both will sever the child's legal relationship with one side of his family, which may be detrimental in emotional and financial terms.[50]   Both also carry the risk of confusion and distress to the child, through the distortion of his relationship, not only with the adopters but also with his parents.   Grandparent adoption, which makes the grandparent a parent and the parent a sibling, is a vivid example of this.   The risk of damage caused by later discovery of the truth might also be greater than in more conventional adoptions.[51]

5.16   Hence the Committee recommended that relatives and step-parents already caring for a child should be able to apply for "guardianship",[52] in order to give them a secure legal status without severing or distorting other relationships.   Adoption should not be banned, because it might be appropriate where the other parent was right out of the picture, but the court should first consider whether guardianship would be better.[53]   No recommendation was made as to the period for which a relative or step-parent should have had care of the child, but at that time an adoption order could not be made unless the child had been with the applicant for at least three months (after the age of six weeks). The Committee expressly rejected any provision for parental consent, as the order could be reviewed at any time and the court would always take the parents' wishes into account.[54]   The Committee might also have

---

49   Ibid., paras. 97 and 111 to 114.

50   Ibid., paras. 111 and 123.

51   Ibid., para. 111.

52   Ibid., para. 120 and recommendation 21.

53   Ibid., paras. 107 to 109 and 112 and recommendation 20.

54   Ibid., para. 125.

observed that it was already possible for step-parents of children whose parents were divorced (and indeed others) to be awarded custody in the divorce proceedings and that in most cases there would be nothing to prevent a parent who objected to the application from removing the child before the hearing.

5.17   Secondly, the Committee had in mind the need to provide security and status for some foster parents, in particular where "the parents are out of the picture, and the foster parents and the child wish to legalise and secure their relationship and be independent of the local authority or child care agency, but the child is old enough to have a sense of identity and wishes to keep this and retain his own name".[55]   There might also be cases where the parents were still in touch but recognised that they would never be able to provide a home for the child.[56]   Finally, some foster parents might not be able to afford to adopt, but could become guardians if financial assistance were available.[57]

5.18   However, although once again the Committee did not propose formal provision for parental consent, some restrictions were recommended in order to spare the parents the anxiety of fruitless applications.   The Committee proposed a qualifying period of twelve

---

55   Ibid., para. 121.

56   Ibid.

57   Ibid.   The views of the Houghton Committee were reinforced by the research carried out by Rowe and Lambert (Children Who Wait (1973)) which showed that of 7,000 children in the long term care of local authorities or voluntary organisations, 5,000 required a secure legal relationship short of adoption which did not entirely sever their links with their natural parents.

months' care, in line with their recommendation for adoption[58] (although it is not clear whether the proposed reduction to three months where the child was placed by an adoption agency[59] was also proposed for guardianship). The parents would retain their right to remove the child beforehand and thus effectively frustrate the application, as would the local authority if the child were in care unless (as was also recommended for adoption) the child had been with the foster parents for five years.[60]

5.19   In the event, while the Committee's recommendations for adoption were implemented without significant change,[61] further qualifications were imposed for "custodianship". It might have been argued that no special qualifications were needed, as the courts would be able to take all the relevant factors into account when deciding what would best promote the child's welfare. However, that would have increased the courts' powers to review the placement decisions made by local authorities. Such an 'open door' might also have added to the concern that parents would lose their confidence in the child care service,[62] and that foster parents (and others) would be encouraged to exclude rather than work with the natural parents, to the detriment of the

---

58   Ibid., para. 122 and recommendation 21.   See also Adoption of Children, Working Paper of the Departmental Committee on the Adoption of Children (1970), paras. 106 to 111.

59   Ibid., para. 91.

60   Ibid., para. 126.

61   In Part I of the Children Act 1975.

62   See, for example, Holman, "Why Custodianship is Such a Paradox", Community Care, 7 May 1975 pp. 18 and 19; and Hansard (H.L.) vol. 356, cols. 25, 64 and 89.

child's relationships and sense of identity.[63] Further, it could have been and subsequently has been argued that if a permanent substitute home is required nothing short of adoption can provide the necessary security and commitment on both sides.[64]

5.20   In the eventual Bill,[65] therefore, it was provided that relatives and step-parents with whom the child had had his home for three months before the application, and others with whom he had lived for a total of twelve months including the preceding three, could apply but only with the consent of a person having legal custody.[66] The periods of care are broadly in line with those required before an adoption order can be made.[67] The requirement of consent was introduced to reassure parents who needed to make use of short term foster care and who might otherwise be deterred from making arrangements which were in their

---

63   Holman, "The Place of Fostering in Social Work", (1975) 5 British Journal of Social Work 3, pp. 8-14, pointed to "inclusive fostering" which draws into the "fostering situation" its component elements including the natural parents.   See also, Holman, "In Defence of Parents", New Society, 1 May 1975 pp. 268 and 269 and Thorpe, "Experience of Children and Parents Living Apart", in Triseliotis (ed.), New Developments in Foster Care and Adoption (1980), pp. 87-95.

64   Adcock, "Alternatives to Adoption", Adoption and Fostering, vol. 8 (1984), pp. 12-15 expressed concern that custodianship would be used to avoid facing up to the painful issues raised by adoption to the ultimate detriment of the child's need for security.

65   The Children Bill, introduced in the House of Lords on 12 December 1974.

66   See C.A. 1975, s. 33(3)(a) and (b).

67   Ibid., s. 9(1) and (2).

children's best interests.[68] It is not clear why the consent of only one person having legal custody was required, for it can scarcely be reassuring to a mother who fosters her child during a period of illness to think that the father could consent to an application. If, on the other hand, it was thought that to require the consent of only one person would "water down" the requirement, it is not clear why it is right to do so where there are two parents with legal custody but not where there is only one.

5.21   There is no provision for dispensing with this consent, save that those shorter qualifying periods apply without the need for consent if there is no person with legal custody or none who can be found.[69] The reasons for these exceptions can readily be understood, but the lack of a dispensing power means that applicants may be able to adopt when they cannot apply for custodianship. This seems contrary to the declared policy of making custodianship more readily available than adoption, as it is so much less final and serious a step for all concerned.[70] One possible reason, however, is that consent is required only to the application for custodianship. Thus the case may proceed even though consent is withdrawn and even, presumably, if a person with legal custody removes the child before the hearing, for the qualifying period would run only up to the making of the application.

5.22   No consent is required, however, if the child has had his home with the applicant for a total of three years, including the previous three months,[71] and where such an application is pending, the child cannot be

---

68   Hansard (H.L.) vol. 356, col. 26 and Hansard (H.C.) vol. 893, col. 1835.

69   C.A. 1975, s. 33(6).

70   Hansard (H.C.) vol. 893, col. 1835.

71   C.A. 1975, s. 33(3)(c).

removed from the applicant without his consent or the court's leave (or other statutory authority).[72] Three years was apparently chosen, instead of the five recommended by the Houghton Committee,[73] because of the less drastic nature of custodianship and in line with the provision (also introduced by the Children Act 1975) allowing local authorities to assume parental rights over children who had been continuously in their care for three years.[74] In the event, however, the position in adoption is often more favourable to the applicants. Although a general prohibition against removal applies (even before an adoption application is made) only when the child has had his home with the applicants for a total of five years, once an application is made to the court, a parent who has given formal agreement to the adoption cannot remove the child without consent or leave of the court,[75] and neither can a local authority which had the child in care.[76]

5.23   Hence it would appear that the qualifications for custodianship do not entirely meet any of their declared objectives. They are not consistently less stringent than those for adoption. They cannot invariably spare parents the pain of unwarranted applications. For example, an application by a relative, such as an aunt, in respect of a niece staying with her during a mother's temporary illness or absence abroad would generally be regarded as unwarranted. Yet the "home"

---

72   Ibid., section 41(1): see para. 2.71 above.

73   Para. 126.

74   See now Child Care Act 1980, s. 3(1)(d).

75   Adoption Act 1958, s. 34: see also Re T. [1986] 1 All E.R. 817.

76   Ibid., ss. 35(2) and 36.

requirement would probably be satisfied and the consent requirement could be supplied by an estranged father who had abandoned the child and mother years earlier. For the same reason, the qualifications cannot reliably reassure parents who make use of the local authority child care service.

5.24   At the same time, while there are obvious advantages in relying on fixed periods of care these can easily be arbitrary or unduly restrictive. It is not obvious, for example, why any distinction should be drawn between relatives and step-parents, on the one hand, and other people. In practice, family friends may have a closer relationship with the child than do aunts and uncles. Furthermore, while "others" may on occasion be local authority foster parents, children in care are also frequently boarded out with relatives. If any distinction between boarded-out children and others is appropriate, therefore, this is not the way to achieve it.

5.25   The qualifications also exclude some applications which might be thought entirely appropriate. For example, where a parent is considering putting a child into local authority care, or fostering him privately, or even placing him for adoption, it may sometimes be quite reasonable for a relative or close family friend to be able to seek custody.

5.26   Finally, these qualifications are difficult to reconcile with the much less stringent requirements where there happen to be other proceedings on foot.   With the current incidence of divorce,[77] the chance of there being proceedings in which an interested party could seek to intervene, perhaps years after the event, are much increased.

---

77   See para. 4.1 above.

Other third parties

5.27   Cases in the 19th century[78] established the courts' powers to grant custody to third parties where matrimonial proceedings were initiated between spouses (who would at that stage also be parents) or Guardianship of Minors Act proceedings between parents.   It would be surprising if a court hearing such a case, and aware that an order in favour of a third party would be the best available means of safeguarding and promoting the child's welfare, were unable to make one.

5.28   Nevertheless, there are still gaps and inconsistencies. Not all proceedings concerning the family or even the upbringing of children enable the court to consider granting custody or access. For example, although injunctions under the Domestic Violence and Matrimonial Proceedings Act 1976 can be granted to protect a child "living with" the applicant, no order can be made about the future upbringing of the child in those proceedings.[79]   Secondly, in some cases the power to make an order depends upon whether or not a financial order or other relief has been granted while in other cases it does not.[80]   Thirdly, as we have already seen, the effect upon parents' rights of an order made in favour of a non-parent differs between the various enactments.[81]

The options for reform

5.29   Given the complete lack of any guiding principle in the present law, it must operate capriciously and so present a strong case for reform. There appear to us to be at least four possible approaches to reform:

---

78   See for example, March v. March and Palumbo (1867) L.R.1 P. & D. 440; Godrich v. Godrich (1873) L.R.3 P. & D. 134 and Chetwynd v. Chetwynd (1865) 4 Sw. & Tr. 151.

79   See para. 2.9 above, and ss. 1(1)(b) & 2(1)(b) of the 1976 Act.

80   See, for example, para. 2.11 above.

81   See paras. 2.16, 2.17 and 2.28 above.

(i)   to extend the rights currently enjoyed by those who have
        treated a child as a member of their family;

(ii)   to rationalise the qualifications for custodianship; and

(iii)   to remove all restrictions on applying for or being
        granted custody or access, but perhaps to impose other
        restrictions in the shape of the grounds upon which
        orders may be made; and in any event

(iv)   to make special provision for children in local authority
        care.

(i) The "child of the family"

5.30   It would now be quite impracticable and unacceptable to turn
back the clock and suggest that courts hearing matrimonial proceedings
should no longer have power to consider and deal with the future of
children other than children of the marriage.   A more practical course
might be to take this development to its logical conclusion and allow any
person to make application for custody of or access to any child who has
been treated as a child of the family in relation to any marriage to which
he has been party, without at the same time having to apply for
matrimonial relief.

5.31   It would, however, be necessary to resolve the present
discrepancy between the 1973 and 1978 Acts as to the effect upon the
position of parents.[82]   Provided that the parents are given an opportunity
of taking part in the proceedings, there seems to be no good reason why
an order should not be binding upon them.   There is little point in

---

82   See paras. 2.16-2.17 above.

determining custody or access between people who otherwise have no claim to it and certainly little logic in the current distinction in the 1973 Act between cases which involve one natural parent and cases which do not. In either case the rights of a person who is not a party to the marriage in question may be affected.

5.32   The impact of such an apparently small development from the existing law would, however, be considerable. There would be little, if any, need to retain the present provision for custodianship, as those who qualify now would almost certainly have treated the child as a member of their family. Indeed, the category of potential applicants would be considerably extended, as it would no longer be necessary that the child "have his home" with the applicant at the time of the application.

5.33   Such a broad qualification would be entirely consistent with the objective of recognising and maintaining those relationships which are (or may be) important to the child, in particular by means of access orders. However, treatment as a member of the family is not a "self-proving" fact so that there would be greater uncertainty for applicants, parents and children alike. It would also be necessary to reconsider the present exclusion of boarded-out children, as custodianship was partly designed with local authority foster parents in mind.[83]   A different approach for them would be consistent, not only with the policy of maintaining confidence in the child care service, but also with the parental responsibilities of the local authorities themselves, and so we shall discuss these children separately.[84]   Finally, it would be necessary to consider whether the concept of treating a child as a member of the

---

83   See paras. 5.17-5.18 above.

84   See paras. 5.41-5.48 below.

family could be extended to single people or unmarried couples. There is no obvious reason why aunts, uncles, grandparents, older brothers or sisters or cohabiting couples should be excluded, as they may well qualify for custodianship.

(ii) The qualified custodian

5.34   There would be fewer anomalies if the qualifications for custodianship approximated more closely to the Houghton Committee's recommendations.[85]   In particular, the removal of any residential qualification for relatives and step-parents would have several advantages.   The discrepancy between "post-death", "post-illegitimacy" and "post-divorce" rights of application by step-parents would be removed.[86]   Step-parenthood is "self-proving", whereas treatment as a child of the family is not; it does not depend upon the attitude of the other spouse, who may have tried to exclude the step-parent from playing any role in relation to the children; it also gives clearer recognition to the role of step-parents who are married to non-custodial parents and who may play a very important part in the children's lives, for example during access visits.   Similar considerations apply to relatives, who presumably often treat a child as a member of their family even if the child is not living with them and may be very well qualified to assume custody in cases of need.

5.35   Similarly, if there were no consent requirement, the curiosities of the current provisions would disappear and the discrepancies between adoption and custodianship would be less apparent.   In practice, there may be little reason to require such consent as a parent who opposes the application can usually remove the child and (in effect if not in law) frustrate matters.   On the other hand, sudden removal will often not be

---

85   See paras. 5.15-5.18 above.

86   See para. 5.14 above.

in the child's best interests, any more than it is just before an arbitrary time limit elapses. While there is little reason to believe that the introduction of time limits in the child care field[87] has led to precipitate actions by parents, notice of an application for custody might be more likely to do so. In an appropriate case, of course, this can already be dealt with by means of an interim order.[88]

5.36   If the qualifications for custodianship were to be relaxed, however, it would be necessary to consider whether special provision were required for children in the care of local authorities. Otherwise, relatives with whom the child was boarded-out might apply immediately and others after, say, twelve months. We discuss these cases separately below.[89]

(iii) An open door

5.37   The simplest way of removing the arbitrariness, gaps and inconsistencies in the present law is to allow non-parents the same rights to apply for custody as have parents. They already have the right to apply for care and control in wardship proceedings, so that no new principle is involved in extending the statutory procedures to them. Given the large numbers of children who have experienced divorce,[90] after which in theory any person can intervene to seek custody (or indeed access), it might not be such a radical step in practice as it at first sight appears.

---

87   Child Care Act 1980, ss. 3(1)(d) and 13(2).

88   See paras. 2.70-2.71 above.

89   Paras. 5.41-5.48 below.

90   See para. 4.1 above.

5.38   It seems that very few people other than parents and spouses are granted custody in divorce proceedings[91] and there is no evidence that third parties abuse their right to intervene in those proceedings. Similarly, apart from local authority cases, only a small proportion of wardships are initiated by non-parents[92] and the number of successful applications by grandparents for access may suggest that they rarely exercise their statutory rights to apply for it.[93] This is scarcely

---

91   Our analysis of statistics provided by the Lord Chancellor's Department revealed that in 1985 at most 400 orders relating to the custody of children made by county court registries in divorce cases were in favour of a person other than a spouse: see the Supplement (op. cit. at n. 17).

92   Our analysis of a sample of 705 1985 wardship cases in the Principal Registry of the Family Division revealed that (apart from the 32.5% of cases initiated by local authorities) only 14.6% of all cases were initiated by a non-parent.   They broke down as follows -

    Grandparents   63 = 61.2%   (8.9% all cases);
    Aunt/Uncle   14 = 13.6%   (2% all cases);
    Foster parents   9 = 8.7%   (1.3% all cases);
    Friends   5 = 4.9%   (0.7% all cases);
    Adoptive parents   3 = 2.9%   (0.4% all cases);
    Step parents   3 = 2.9%   (0.4% all cases);
    Second cousin   1 = 1.0%   (0.1% all cases);
    Cohabitee   1 = 1.0%   (0.1% all cases);
    Health authority   1 = 1.0%   (0.1% all cases);
    Step parent   1 = 1.0%   (0.1% all cases);
    Half brother   1 = 1.0%   (0.1% all cases); and
    Other   1 = 1.0%   (0.1% all cases):
    TOTAL   103   (14.6% all cases)

93   In 1984, only 100 orders were made in magistrates' courts granting access to grandparents under section 14 of the Domestic Proceedings and Magistrates' Courts Act 1978 and section 14A of the Guardianship of Minors Act 1971 (Home Office Statistical Bulletin, Issue 24/85); and our analysis of statistics provided by the Lord Chancellor's Department shows that in the county courts in 1985 only 21 access orders were granted to grandparents under section 14A of the 1971 Act: see the Supplement to this paper (op. cit. at n. 17).

surprising, as few would be anxious to take the speculative and sometimes costly step of litigation without a very good reason, nor would those who required it be granted legal aid unless they could demonstrate that there were reasonable grounds for the action.[94]

5.39   It may therefore be that a requirement of leave, which currently applies to most interventions in divorce suits,[95] would be a sufficient deterrent against unwarranted applications and would allow the court to judge whether the applicant stood a reasonable prospect of success in the light of all the circumstances of the case. The application could be made ex parte to prevent unnecessary disturbance to a family's life where the action was clearly unmeritorious. Such requirements are familiar in the High Court and county courts and by no means unknown in the magistrates' domestic jurisdiction.[96] The arbitrariness of the present law would thus be avoided and a few children might benefit as a result.

---

94   Section 7(5) and (5A) of the Legal Aid Act 1974 provides that

"A person shall not be given legal aid ... unless he shows that he has reasonable grounds for taking, defending or being a party [to proceedings]"

and

"A person may be refused legal aid if ... it appears -

(a)   unreasonable that he should receive it ...".

95   See para. 2.18 above.

96   For example, the statute leaves it to the court to decide, in effect, whether to entertain the prospect of granting legal custody to a third party under section 8(3) of the Domestic Proceedings and Magistrates' Courts Act 1978 when hearing an application for financial relief under that Act. See also, for example, section 37(1) and (3) of the Children Act 1975.

There would, however, be some risk of inconsistencies between different courts, perhaps even that some would take a more restrictive approach than the present law.

5.40   Once again, however, special consideration must be given to the case of local authority foster parents.   An unrestricted right of access to the courts would be a new departure in principle for them, as the High Court has consistently refused to allow them to use the wardship procedure in order to challenge the placement decisions of local authorities.[97]   Only if the local authority is effectively out of the picture,[98] or has asked for the court's aid,[99] may the wardship jurisdiction be invoked, not only by foster parents but also by anyone else in respect of a child in local authority care.[100]

(iv) Children in care

5.41   As already seen, children in care are treated differently from others in both the matrimonial and wardship jurisdictions and the restrictions in custodianship have been devised partly with their special circumstances in mind.   Most children are received into care under section 2 of the Child Care Act 1980 without any compulsory measures against them or their parents.   It is important to maintain the confidence of parents in this system and indeed the Review of Child Care Law has

---

97   Re M. [1961] Ch. 328; Re T. (A.J.J.) [1970] Ch. 688.

98   Re J. [1984] 1 All E.R. 29.

99   Re G. [1963] 1 W.L.R. 1169; Re B. [1975] Fam. 36.

100 See Re H. [1978] Fam. 65; M. v. Humberside County Council [1979] Fam. 114; Re W. [1980] Fam. 60; A. v. Liverpool City Council [1982] A.C. 363, Re W. [1985] A.C. 791. The same reasoning applies when care proceedings are pending: Re E. (1983) 4 F.L.R. 668, and even when a local authority is simply intending to take the child into care: W. v. Nottinghamshire County Council (1985) The Times, 16 November 1985.

made several recommendations designed, not only to increase the degree of partnership between parents and local authorities[101] but also to extend the same legal provisions to other children who are living away from home in local authority accommodation but not technically in care.[102] Under the present law, the local authority can only acquire the parents' rights by means of care proceedings[103] or the procedure for assuming parental rights by resolution;[104] in both cases specific conditions have to be fulfilled in addition to the general welfare test.[105] Under the Review's recommendations, local authorities would only compulsorily acquire parental rights if they could show, not only that they could do better than the parents, but also that the child was suffering or was likely to suffer harm as a result of shortcomings in his home.[106] It would therefore be surprising if local authority foster parents could acquire the parental right of custody more readily than could the authority.

---

101   Review of Child Care Law ("R.C.C.L.") (1985), Chs. 7 and 9.

102   Ibid., Ch. 4.

103   Children and Young Persons Act 1969, s. 1.

104   Child Care Act 1980, s. 3.

105   In care proceedings under section 1 of the Children and Young Persons Act 1969 the court, having satisfied itself that the conditions for an order exist may, "if it thinks fit" make one of the available orders. That final discretion appears to be governed by the welfare principle in section 1 of the Guardianship of Minors Act 1971 which requires the child's welfare to be treated as the "first and paramount" consideration (Re C (1981) 2 F.L.R. 62, 65). In parental rights resolution cases under section 3 of the Child Care Act 1980 the local authority in deciding whether to pass a resolution must give only "first consideration to the need to safeguard and promote the welfare of the child...". However, if a resolution is challenged in court, the court may only confirm the resolution if "it is in the interests of the child to do so" (section 3(6)(c)), which the Review of Child Care Law considered "has a similar effect to applying section 1 of the 1971 Act": (op. cit. at n. 101), para. 15.7.

106   R.C.C.L. (ibid.), para. 15.25.

5.42   The unqualified right in foster parents to apply for custody could also be seen as an unprecedented interference in the child care responsibilities of the local authority. As has recently been emphasised, both by the Review of Child Care Law and by the report of the inquiry team in the Jasmine Beckford case, it is important to strengthen rather than to undermine the responsibility of local authorities to make the best possible provision for each child in their care.[107]   If foster parents were able to challenge their placement decisions in the courts, there would clearly be even greater pressure to allow parents to do so.

5.43   The custodianship provisions were clearly influenced by such considerations, although it was decided not to impose any special requirements for children in care.   Indeed, recent research[108] into long term fostering suggests that few local authority foster parents will see custodianship as a desirable solution.   There will be some financial sacrifice, unless the authority decide to continue the full boarding-out allowance.[109]   Like step-parents after divorce, they may also be reluctant to go through an intrusive and speculative legal procedure for advantages which are not so readily understood as are those of adoption.[110]

5.44   A further consideration is that the Review of Child Care Law has recommended that custodianship and adoption be used, instead of the

---

107   Ibid., paras. 2.24, 8.3 and 8.12: and A Child in Trust (1985), pp. 16 and 21.

108   Rowe, Cain, Hundleby and Keane, Long Term Foster Care (1984), pp. 152, 171 and 200 to 201.

109   C.A. 1975 s. 34(6).

110   Masson, Norbury and Chatterton, Mine, Yours or Ours? (1983), p. 85 and Priest, "Step-parent Adoptions: What is the Law?" [1982] J.S.W.L. 285, 291.

assumption of parental rights by resolution, to provide a secure and permanent home for children in care who could not in future be the subject of care proceedings because they are not at risk of harm from their parents.[111] A substantial relaxation in the present qualifications for custodianship would therefore have a greater impact upon the child care system than might otherwise have been the case.

5.45   It would, of course, produce further inconsistency if under an "open door" policy people who were not already caring for a child could apply to the courts but foster parents of children in care could not do so. Nevertheless the considerations above are sufficiently powerful to persuade us that some restriction in the case of children in care must be retained.

5.46   In devising such a restriction, first consideration should be given to the welfare of the children involved. The security and stability which might be gained from a custodianship order must be set against the difficulties which premature applications might cause in the making and realisation of the local authority's plans, particularly for children who have been compulsorily removed from inadequate homes. Current child care practice places great emphasis upon planning a secure and permanent home for children who might otherwise have to grow up in care. This may be achieved either through making strenuous efforts to solve the family's problems and reach a position where parents and child may be reunited or through finding an alternative family which can provide the sort of care which is best suited to the child's needs. Such plans may obviously take some time to formulate and put into effect. The risks of deterring parents from using the voluntary child care service and resorting to other arrangements which may be much less satisfactory

---

111   R.C.C.L. (op. cit. at n. 101), paras. 15.28 to 15.33.

must also be borne in mind.   Neither problem arises where the local authority or, where the child is in voluntary care, the parents, have given their consent to the application.

5.47   Where such consent is not forthcoming, however, the present law requires that the child has had his home with the applicants for a total of three years.   There is always a risk in any arbitrary time limit that the child will be prematurely removed in order to frustrate a possible application, thus destroying the very security which the procedure is intended to confer.   We do not believe, however, that any local authority would terminate an otherwise satisfactory and stable placement for such a reason nor does experience of the time limits introduced into child care law by the 1975 Act suggest that parents would be tempted to do so.   The period of residence must therefore be such as to suggest that the application might have a chance of success, even without the consent of parent or local authority, sufficient to justify any possible interference with the authority's plans, particularly for reuniting the child with his family, or damage to the parents' confidence in the system.   The present period of three years is so long in the life of a child, particularly a young child, that an application is almost bound to succeed.   Bearing in mind that the local authority will always report to the court and be a party to the proceedings, there may well be a case for reducing the period to one year where there may still be a good chance that it will be in the child's best interests for an order to be made.

5.48   Hence we provisionally propose that the foster parents of a child who has been boarded out by a local authority should be able to apply (a) with the consent of the local authority if the child is in compulsory care, or (b) with the consent of each parent if the child is in voluntary care under section 2 of the Child Care Act 1980.[112]   Where no

---

112   It has been recommended that "shared care" replace reception into voluntary care under section 2: R.C.C.L. (ibid.), Ch. 7.

such consent is given, we would welcome views upon (a) whether the period for which the child has had his home with the applicants could be reduced from three years, and (b) if so, whether to one or to two years, or indeed to any other period.

Two possible alternatives

5.49 Instead of restricting the circumstances in which non-parents may apply for custody, it might be possible to achieve similar objectives:

(i) by imposing a substantive consent requirement, similar to that in adoption, which could be dispensed with on similar grounds;[113] or

(ii) by requiring grounds other than the "first and paramount consideration" of the child's welfare.[114]

5.50 The advantage of a substantive consent requirement is that it would provide apparently better protection to parents, while a dispensing power would avoid the arbitrariness of the present conditions. The most common ground for dispensing with parental agreement to adoption is that it is being unreasonably withheld.[115] Whereas parents may be quite reasonable in refusing to agree to the total severance of legal ties with children who are being brought up by someone else, it is much more difficult to see how they could be reasonable in withholding agreement to a custody order when it was in the child's best interests to remain where

---

113 C.A. 1975, s. 12 [Adoption Act 1976, s. 16].

114 G.M.A. 1971, s. 1.

115 Second Report to Parliament on the Children Act 1975 (1984/85) (H.C. 20).

he was. Yet it would be difficult to justify having grounds for dispensing with consent to custodianship which were different from or more stringent than those for adoption.

5.51   It is much more tempting to suggest that, in principle, the grounds for depriving a parent of custody in favour of a third party should be the same as those for depriving him of similar parental rights in favour of a local authority.   Were the grounds for care proceedings recommended by the Review of Child Care Law[116] to prove acceptable, this approach would have much to commend it where non-parents were seeking to remove a child from unsatisfactory parents or to prevent a child returning to them.   It would not, however, provide a solution to the problem for which custodianship was primarily designed, of the need to formalise and secure a relationship between the child and his "psychological parents"[117] even though this is not at present threatened by his natural parents.   Furthermore, given that the courts have been able to apply the welfare principle in such cases for at least 15 years,[118] it would be difficult to deny them the power to do what they thought best for the child in the future.   We return to this question in Part VI.

B.   **The orders available**

5.52   The present scheme of orders available when awarding custody to non-parents is subject to exactly the same criticisms as that available between parents.[119]   There is inconsistency between the Matrimonial

---

116   R.C.C.L. (op. cit. at n. 101), para. 15.25.

117   Goldstein, Freud and Solnit, Beyond the Best Interests of the Child (1973), pp. 17-20.

118   J. v. C. [1970] A.C. 668.

119   See paras. 4.22-4.26 and 2.34-2.50 above.

Causes Act and the other enactments and doubt about the meaning of "custody" under the former in particular. Under the other enactments, non-parents (apart from spouses involved in matrimonial proceedings) can only be awarded legal custody by way of a custodianship order. This means that there is only one "bundle of powers" which may be granted to them and that parents cannot be allowed to retain specified rights to share with them.[120]

5.53   There is, however, one major difference between parents and non-parents, in that non-parents have no parental powers and responsibilities unless and until they are awarded some by a court. The options for reform cannot, therefore, be identical to those canvassed for parents.[121] Once again, three possibilities arise:

(i)   a completely flexible approach;

(ii)   clarification and modification of the existing orders; and

(iii)   a new scheme to complement that for parents.

5.54   Objections to a completely flexible approach in this context are just as powerful as they are between parents,[122] and the risks of inconsistency are probably greater.

5.55   The main features of the existing scheme could be retained, in that custody could be granted to sole or joint custodians, giving them powers of action over most aspects of the child's upbringing, while access

---

120   C.A. 1975, s. 44: see also paras. 2.29 and 2.49 above.

121   See paras. 4.47-57 above.

122   See para. 4.48 above.

could be granted to parents. Possible modifications would include the power to spell out in the order certain steps which could not be taken (such as changing the child's surname or taking him abroad) without leave of the court or parental consent,[123] or, more significantly, a power to order that parents retain specified rights, apart from the right to actual custody, holding them jointly with the custodian.[124] Thus a grandmother could be granted custody of her grandchild, but the mother might also retain her voice in the more strategic decisions in that child's life, as under a divorce court joint custody order between parents.[125]

5.56   This approach assumes, as does the Children Act 1975,[126] that the person granted actual custody should always have legal custody, even if some strategic powers may be shared with another person. There could be a case for distinguishing between parents and non-parents, and allowing courts simply to grant actual custody or care and control to a non-parent, leaving longer-term decisions to the parents or a local authority having parental rights. We believe, however, that this would not be satisfactory, as it is so difficult to separate the responsibilities of day-to-day care from the longer-term decisions which are also required.

5.57   More difficult is whether the scheme for sharing out the child's time[127] which we have canvassed for parents might also be used where non-parents are involved. There are obviously attractions in doing

---

123   As in divorce cases: see paras. 2.51 and 2.58 and 2.59 above.

124   As in G.M.A. 1971, s. 11A(1) and D.P.M.C.A. 1978, s. 8(4); see paras. 2.45-2.47 above.

125   See paras. 2.42-2.44 and 4.35-4.43 above.

126   Section 44(1).

127   Paras. 4.51-4.57 above.

so where the court is asked to give joint custody to a parent and step-parent following divorce. It would be necessary, however, not only to grant the step-parent care and control but also to clarify his parental status. One means of doing this would be guardianship,[128] which carries with it almost all the powers and responsibilities of parenthood.[129]

5.58   The Houghton Committee itself recommended the use of the term "guardianship" for what subsequently became custodianship,[130] although it clearly had in mind the extension of the courts' powers to award custody rather than appoint guardians. The difference is that custodians have no powers over the child's property,[131] nor do they acquire exactly the same statutory position as a guardian: for example, their consent is required to the child's marriage,[132] but not to his adoption.[133] There is much to be said for employing the concept of guardianship for all non-parents who stand in the place of parents, although it may also be appropriate to allow the court to limit their powers over certain matters (such as property) in individual cases.[134]

---

128   Working Paper No. 91, paras. 4.15-4.19 and 4.32-39.

129   Ibid., paras. 2.21-2.35.

130   Op. cit. at n. 47, Ch. 6; see also Working Paper No. 91, para. 4.38.

131   See the definition of legal custody in s. 86 C.A. 1975 and paras. 2.40-2.41 above; the Government was concerned that guardianship "would give rise to many problems regarding property law and other matters": Standing Committee A, 24 July 1975 (1974-1975) vol. 1, col. 504; c.f. Bevan and Parry, Children Act 1975 (1979), para. 206.

132   See para. 2.52 above and Marriage Act 1949, Second Schedule, Part I.

133   C.A. 1975, s. 12(1)(b) [Adoption Act 1976, s. 16(1)(b)].

134   See Working Paper No. 91, paras. 3.2-3.6, 3.82-3.85 and Part IV generally.

5.59   Under this approach, therefore, non-parents would be granted guardianship of the child.   The court would be able to place specific limitations on their powers.   It would also be able to order that some or all powers should be retained by the parents and shared with the guardian and further that the parents should have temporary care and control during access visits.

5.60   This scheme could be as appropriate for step-parents who share care and control with one of the parents as for other types of custodian.   It could also be accompanied by the scheme for private appointments of guardians to share a sole parent's status which was canvassed in our earlier paper on Guardianship.[135]

C. Access

5.61   The present powers of the courts to grant access to non-parents are, if anything, even more arbitrary than their powers to grant custody.[136]   The current restrictions in the rights of grandparents to apply for access are particularly difficult to defend.[137]   Indeed, once a right of access is granted to any person other than a parent, there is no logical stopping-place short of allowing it to all those with whom it is in the interests of the child to keep in touch.   On the other hand, there may be a much greater risk that parents will be troubled by unwarranted claims for access than for custody, so that some restriction to the people most likely to be important to the child may be desirable.   The obvious candidates are those who have treated the child as a member of their

---

135   Working Paper No. 91, paras. 4.9-4.31.

136   See paras. 2.55-2.57 above.

137   Paras. 2.20, 2.21 and 2.23 above.

family, including any who have previously had custody under a court order, and relatives within the current definition (i.e. grandparents, brothers and sisters, uncles and aunts).[138]   The very little use which is made of the present powers indicates that parents would have little to fear from such an extension.

5.62   If our new approach to the allocation of custody between parents were accepted, it would be necessary to decide whether access by non-parents should, as we have proposed as between parents, also be classified as temporary care and control.   Without the accompanying parental status, which would enhance the responsibilities of a parent during access, the position of non-parents would be little different from the present.   There may well, however, be advantages in drawing a clear distinction between people who have some responsibility for a child's upbringing and those who merely wish to retain some contact with the child.   For the most part, the child will be seeing these people because it is in his interests to see them, and not because it is in his interests that they maintain a parental responsibility for his future.   In our view, therefore, a simple visiting order would be more appropriate.

D.   Conclusion

5.63   We hesitate to make proposals for reform when changes first provided for in 1975 have only just been brought into force.   Nevertheless, some conclusions seem to us justified:

> (i)   There is little reason to believe that to allow non-parents wishing for custody open access to the courts, perhaps with a requirement of leave, would expose parents or children to any significant risk of unwarranted

---

138   See Adoption Act 1958, s. 60; C.A. 1975, s. 107(1) and para. 2.27 above.

applications, but there is a good case for making special provision for children in local authority care and we would welcome views as to the precise form which this should take.[139]

(ii) There are good grounds for suggesting that the present confusion of orders should be replaced with a single scheme allowing courts to appoint non-parents guardians, perhaps with additional powers both to impose specific limitations and to order the retention of certain responsibilities (including temporary care and control) by the parents.

(iii) There is a good case for confining the concept of access by non-parents (unless they are also guardians) to visiting rights, but the courts' powers to make a visiting order could be severed from their present connection with other proceedings and extended to relatives as well as to those who have treated the child as a member of their family.

5.64 Such a scheme would be capable of applying to all the current cases in which custody or access may be granted to non-parents and would therefore represent a considerable simplification in a complex area.

---

139 See paras. 5.46-5.48 above.

PART VI

THE WELFARE PRINCIPLE

A. The present law

6.1   Section 1 of the Guardianship of Minors Act 1971 provides that:

> ".... Where in any proceedings before any court ...
> (a)   the legal custody or upbringing of a minor; or
> (b)   the administration of any property belonging to or held on trust for a minor, or the application of the income thereof,
> is in question, the court, in deciding that question, shall regard the welfare of the minor as the first and paramount consideration, and shall not take into consideration whether from any other point of view the claim of the father, in respect of such legal custody, upbringing, administration or application is superior to that of the mother, or the claim of the mother is superior to that of the father."

This lays down the basic rule that courts are under a duty to further the "best interests" of the child.

6.2   The origins of this provision lie in the equitable jurisdiction of the Court of Chancery, where the judges tentatively began to develop it during the late 18th and 19th centuries, for example, in relation to the appointment and removal of guardians[1] and the denial of custody to a father on grounds of unfitness or inability.[2] This trend coincided

---

1   Johnstone v. Beattie (1843) 10 Cl. & Fin. 42, 152 per Lord Langdale; Stuart v. Marquis of Bute (1861) 9 H.L.C. 440, 464 per Lord Campbell L.C., 472 per Lord Wensleydale, 474 per Lord Chelmsford; Re McGrath [1893] 1 Ch. 143, 148 per Lord Lindley.

2   Powel v. Cleaver (1789) 2 Bro C.C. 499; Creuze v. Hunter (1790) 2 Cox 242; Ex p. Warner (1792) 4 Bro. C.C. 101; Wellesley v. Beaufort (1827) 2 Russ 1; Anon (1851) 2 Sim. (N.S.) 54.

with the development of remedies whereby the mother of a legitimate child could claim custody or access from the father.[3] The welfare of the child was first prescribed by statute as a relevant consideration, along with the conduct and wishes of the parents, in the Guardianship of Infants Act 1886.[4] It was subsequently held that this placed mother and father on an equal footing in the allocation of custody between them.[5] The Guardianship of Infants Act 1925 completed this trend, by proclaiming the equality of the mother's and father's claims and formulating the welfare test in its present language. This test was later held to be declaratory of the then existing law, not only as between the parents of a legitimate child, but also as between parents and others.[6]

6.3   Hence, the idea that the child's welfare could override parental claims was at once the cause and effect of two other developments. One was equality between the parents. When mothers were first permitted to seek custody or access from fathers, it was the welfare of the child rather than the claims of the mother which became the justification for interfering with his rights.[7] Once mothers had

---

3   Custody of Infants Acts 1839 and 1873, Matrimonial Causes Acts 1857 and 1878, Guardianship of Infants Act 1886.

4   Section 5; since consolidated as section 9(1), Guardianship of Infants Act 1971.

5   Re A. and B. [1897] 1 Ch. 786.

6   J. v. C. [1970] A.C. 668 relying, inter alia, on the contemporaneous appeal to the House of Lords in the Irish case of Ward v. Laverty [1925] AC 101, 108 in which Viscount Cave stated that

     "the wishes of the father only prevail if they are not displaced by considerations relating to the welfare of the children themselves".

7   Re Flynn (1848) 2 De G. and Sm. 457, 474 per Lord Knight Bruce; Re Curtis (1859) 28 L.J. Ch. 458.

achieved fully equal status, however, the same criterion could be employed for judging between the parents. In matrimonial disputes, the courts were for some time inclined to regard matrimonial conduct as the deciding factor, but in the course of the 20th century it was recognised that priority should be given to the children's interests over those of the adults.[8] This in itself may be attributed to the second development, which was the recognition of the status of the child as a person in his own right, rather than the object of the rights of others.[9] The 19th century had seen a growing awareness of the need, not only to protect children from the abuses to which they might be subjected both at home and in the outside world,[10] but also to provide them with the education and other care required for them to become healthy and useful members of society.[11] It was not only in their interests but also in those of society as a whole to promote their welfare, sometimes at the expense of the welfare or wishes of their parents. The welfare principle or variations of it has been widely adopted in other common law jurisdictions, in the

---

8   For the development of the law see Clout v. Clout and Hollebone (1861) 2 Sw. & Tr. 391; Bent v. Bent and Footman (1861) 2 Sw. and Tr. 392; Re A. and B. [1897] 1 Ch. D. 786; Mozley-Stark v. Mozley-Stark and Hitchins [1910] P. 190; Allen v. Allen [1948] 2 All E.R. 413; Willoughby v. Willoughby [1951] P. 14; Wakeham v. Wakeham [1954] 1 W.L.R. 366; Re K. [1977] Fam. 179.

9   See Freeman, The Rights and Wrongs of Children (1984), Ch. 1, for the evolution of this concept.

10   As demonstrated by, e.g. the Infant Life Protection Act 1872, Prevention of Cruelty to and Protection of Children Act 1889, Prevention of Cruelty to Children Act 1904, Children Act 1908 and Children and Young Persons Act 1933.

11   As demonstrated by, e.g. the Elementary Education Acts 1870 and 1876 and the Maternity and Child Welfare Act 1918.

United States and the Commonwealth and also within Western Europe. The Council of Europe has recently reaffirmed that "the welfare of the child is of overriding importance in reaching decisions concerning his custody".[12]

When does section 1 apply?

6.4   Section 1 governs any proceedings in which the legal custody or upbringing of the child or the administration of a child's property is in question, including wardship cases and matrimonial causes (principally divorce), disputes under the Guardianship Acts, the matrimonial jurisdiction of magistrates,[13] and in custodianship proceedings.[14] Although section 1 refers to proceedings in which certain matters in relation to the child are "in question", the paramountcy rule is not only applicable in cases of dispute.   It applies equally, for example, in exercising the statutory duties imposed by section 41 of the Matrimonial Causes Act 1973 in reviewing the arrangements for children after divorce and in considering whether or not to make a custody or access order under section 8(1) of the Domestic Proceedings and Magistrates' Courts Act 1978.

---

12   The preamble to the European Convention on Recognition and Enforcement of Decisions Concerning Custody of Children and on Restoration of Custody of Children (20 May 1980).   Further, "any decision of the competent authority concerning the attribution of parental responsibilities or the way in which these responsibilities are exercised should be based primarily on the interests of the child", Principle 2 of Parental Responsibilities, Recommendation No. R(84)4 adopted by the Committee of Ministers of the Council of Europe on 28 February 1984.

13   D.P.M.C.A. 1978, s. 15.

14   C.A. 1975, s. 33(9).

6.5   Even within matrimonial disputes, however, it was held in Richards v. Richards[15] that the paramountcy rule will only apply where the child's welfare is "directly in question". The House of Lords, by a majority, decided that in an application for an ouster injunction, the upbringing of a child was only an incidental matter, and was only one of the factors to be considered by the court, as provided by section 1(3) of the Matrimonial Homes Act 1983. Lord Scarman, dissenting, held that the paramountcy rule should be applied because the making of an ouster order could not be considered without having regard to the question of custody. The welfare test does not, moreover, permit the courts to review the exercise of the statutory powers of local authorities[16] and considerations of public policy may dictate a course of action other than that which is strictly best for the child.[17]

6.6   In our Report on Illegitimacy we have recommended[18] that it should be made clear that the welfare test applies to non-marital children in the same way as to marital children, thus putting beyond doubt that the legal relationship between a child's parents is irrelevant in determining what is the child's best interests.   That Report also recommends[19] that the provision in section 9(1) of the 1971 Act, requiring the court to have regard to the conduct and wishes of the father and mother as well as the welfare of the child be removed and with it any gloss on the paramountcy rule.

---

15   [1984] A.C. 174, 223 per Lord Brandon.

16   A. v. Liverpool City Council [1982] A.C. 363; Re W [1985] A.C. 791.

17   Re Mohamed Arif [1968] 1 Ch. 643, and Re X. [1975] Fam. 47.

18   (1982) Law Com. No. 118, paras. 7.22-7.23 and Cl. 2 of the Family Law Reform Bill annexed.

19   Ibid., paras. 7.23-24 and Cl. 5 of the Family Law Reform Bill.

6.7   The duty laid down in section 1 is vested in the court. However, recent dicta have suggested that first and paramount consideration must also be given to the child's welfare by parents, irrespective of court proceedings. Thus Lord Scarman in Gillick v. West Norfolk and Wisbech Health Authority said that "parental right must be exercised in accordance with the welfare principle and can be challenged, even overridden, if it be not".[20] As we have already indicated,[21] in practice there are limits to what can be expected of parents in everyday life. Nor is there power under the custody jurisdictions, with which we are concerned in this paper, to submit single issues of upbringing for decision by the courts, save between parents or those who hold custody jointly.[22] It is clear, however, that the welfare test will apply to the resolution of those issues.

6.8   Section 1 also applies to care proceedings once the statutory pre-conditions in section 1 of the Children and Young Persons Act 1969 have been fulfilled.[23] Section 3 of the Children Act 1975 lays down a

---

20   [1986] A.C. 112, 184.

21   See para. 3.2 above.

22   G.A. 1973, s. 1(3); C.A. 1975, s. 38; D.P.M.C.A. 1978, s. 13(1).

23   Re C. (1979) 2 F.L.R. 62, 65; s. 44(1) of the Children and Young Persons Act 1933 applies where a child is brought before the court in care proceedings, but has apparently been overtaken by the paramountcy rule, which expressly applies as to access to children in care: Child Care Act 1980, s. 12F(1).   If the statutory preconditions cannot be fulfilled, local authorities may resort to wardship to secure the welfare of the child, Re C.B. [1981] 1 W.L.R. 379 and Hertfordshire County Council v. Dolling (1981) 3 F.L.R. 423.

different criterion for adoption.[24]   In criminal cases it seems that section 44(1) of the Children and Young Persons Act 1933, which provides for "regard" to be had to the child's welfare, is intended to provide room for the public interest in controlling criminal activity to outweigh what may be best for the individual child.[25]

What does the rule mean?

6.9   The most often quoted exposition of the paramountcy rule is that of Lord MacDermott in J. v. C..[26]   It means

> "more than that the child's welfare is to be treated as the top item in a list of items relevant to the matters in question. [The words] connote a process whereby, when all the relevant facts, relationships, claims and wishes of parents, risks, choices and other circumstances are taken into account and weighed, the course to be followed will be that which is most in the interests of the child's welfare as that term has now to be understood. That is the first consideration because it is of first importance and the paramount consideration because it rules upon or determines the course to be followed".

His Lordship therefore makes it plain that the decision of the court must be "that which is most in the interests of the child's welfare". Hence the court need only take into account considerations which are relevant to the child's welfare and all other factors, including the way in which married parents have behaved towards one another, are relevant only insofar as

---

24   That "... first consideration (be) given to the need to safeguard and promote the welfare of the child throughout his childhood ..."   The presence of two tests, giving different weight to the child's welfare, may cause difficulty.   In Re C. (1979) 2 F.L.R. 177, where the court had to consider the adoption of a child in wardship proceedings, the approach taken was to do what was in the best interests of the child and the difference between the tests was not considered.

25   See Lord Wilberforce in A. v. Liverpool City Council [1982] A.C. 363, 372.

26   J. v. C. [1970] A.C. 668, 710-711.

they cast light upon that welfare.[27]   In other words the rule of paramountcy must be applied "without qualification, compromise or gloss".[28]   Previously, the additional use of the word "first" had led some courts to believe that they might balance other considerations against the welfare of the child, but since J. v. C. that view does not seem to be tenable.[29]   "First" is therefore now superfluous and its retention could cause confusion.[30]

6.10   The welfare of the child is to be assessed in its widest sense. In 1893, it was said that:

> "the welfare of the child is not to be measured by money alone nor by physical comfort only ....   The moral and religious welfare of the child must be considered as well as its physical well-being.   Nor can the ties of affection be disregarded".[31]

---

27   S. (B.D.) v. S. (D.J.) [1977] Fam. 109.

28   Re C. (1979) 2 F.L.R. 177, 184 per Roskill L.J.; see also Danckwerts L.J. in Re Adoption Application No. 41/61 [1963] 1 Ch. 315, 329.

29   See e.g. Re Thain [1926] Ch. 676, Re L. [1962] 1 W.L.R. 886 and Re F. [1969] 2 Ch 238, 241; c.f. Re K. [1977] Fam. 179 and S. (B.D.) v. S. (D.J.) [1977] Fam. 109.

30   In the Australian Family Law Act 1975 the word "first" was omitted. Section 23(1) of the Guardianship Act 1968 in New Zealand restricts the court's cognisance of parental conduct "to the extent only that such conduct is relevant to the welfare of the child."   The English formula has been described as an example of "draftsman's duplicity (now obsolete)": Bennion, "First Consideration: A Cautionary Tale" (1976) 126 N.L.J. 1237.

31   Lindley L.J. in Re McGrath [1893] 1 Ch. 143, 148. In Re A. [1963] 1 W.L.R. 231, 234 Cross J. equated welfare with "benefit", although material benefit will usually be of "little weight": Stephenson v. Stephenson [1985] F.L.R. 1140, 1148 per Wood J.

More recent accounts would give much greater weight to the ties of affection, as in this example from New Zealand:

> "'Welfare' is an all-encompassing word. It includes material welfare, both in the sense of an adequacy of resources to provide a pleasant home and a comfortable standard of living and in the sense of an adequacy of care to ensure that good health and due personal pride are maintained. However, while material considerations have their place, they are secondary matters. More important are the stability and the security, the loving and understanding care and guidance, the warm and compassionate relationships, that are essential for the full development of the child's own character, personality and talents."[32]

6.11　　A child's welfare may be viewed in the long and short term. Section 1 refers to a "minor" and reported cases clearly concentrate on both the immediate ties and environment of the child. They do anticipate future contingencies such as parental acquisition of employment[33] and remarriage.[34] As to the child's own development, regard will be had to furthering his character and education.[35] The position was summarised thus in an Australian case:

> "There will be cases where the extreme youth of the child gives immediacy to the parental bond ... (and) where illness or temporary separation require an order geared to a short term. Where however, the child is beyond the stage of babyhood and is capable of forming those relationships which will give it 'a good start in life', the court is obliged to attempt predictions into the longer term".[36]

32　Hardie Boys J. in Walker v. Walker and Harrison noted in [1981] N.Z. Recent Law 257.

33　E.g. B. v. B. [1985] F.L.R. 462 and Re D.W. (1983) 14 Fam. Law 17.

34　E.g. S. (B.D.) v. S. (D.J.) [1977] Fam. 109.

35　E.g. May v. May [1986] F.L.R. 325.

36　Raby and Raby (1976) 12 A.L.R. 669, 679.

Other provisions[37] refer to the need to safeguard and promote the child's welfare "throughout his childhood", but decisions taken during childhood may clearly be designed to promote his welfare as an adult. Indeed, the paramountcy rule suggests that, for as long as he is a child, he should be given the best opportunity to develop his own potential, even if the benefit will be enjoyed when he is adult and at some cost to other adults, in particular his parents.

6.12   Beyond that, it is not necessary for us to go for the purposes of the present discussion. There are, of course, many reported decisions casting light upon the factors to be taken into account in assessing a child's welfare.[38]   In some, there may be detected a tendency to develop "rules of thumb" as to what course will indeed be most in the interests of a particular child's welfare.[39]   Nevertheless, it has frequently been stressed that there are no other rules:

> "although one may of course be assisted by the wisdom of remarks made in earlier cases, the circumstances in infant cases and the personalities of the parties concerned being infinitely variable, the conclusions of the court as to the course which should be followed in one case are of little assistance in guiding one to the course which ought to be followed in another case."[40]

---

37   C.A. 1975, s. 3 [Adoption Act 1976, s. 6];   Child Care Act 1980, s. 18(1).

38   See Cretney, Principles of Family Law 4th ed. (1984), ch. 12.

39   For example in cases concerned with a mother's claim for custody of younger children see Re K. [1977] Fam. 179, 189 per Stamp L.J. and at p. 191 per Ormrod L.J.   See also L. v. L. (1980) 2 F.L.R. 48, Plant v. Plant (1982) 4 F.L.R. 305, Re W. (1982) 4 F.L.R. 492, Bowley v. Bowley [1984] F.L.R. 791, Pountney v. Morris [1984] F.L.R. 381, B. v. B. [1985] F.L.R. 166 and Stephenson v. Stephenson [1985] F.L.R. 1140.

40   Re K. [1977] Fam. 179, 183 per Stamp L.J.

B. Is paramountcy the right rule?

6.13   The present rule gives absolute priority to the welfare of the child. Although the courts will take account of a wide range of matters for their bearing on the child's interests, the absolute standard could in theory produce results which might be considered undesirable. If the interests of the child before the court are given priority over the interests of other children, other members of his family and the public, a relatively minor advantage for that child would have to be pursued by the court in spite of what may be seriously deleterious consequences for other people. It might, for example, be marginally better for a child to be brought up by his father and step-mother, but the resulting hurt and loss to his mother could be devastating.   In practice, the strength of the mother's feelings and commitment would be an important factor in the child's welfare. Moreover it may not be in the child's interests for serious harm to another to be caused to promote his own slight advantage.   It may be, therefore, that so stark a dilemma will rarely arise.

6.14   As we have already seen,[41] the claims of each parent are now assumed to be equal before the court.   We could not suggest that the law should return to its former preference for the claims of the father.   Nor would we suggest that the claims of the mother should be given any greater priority than they tend already to enjoy by virtue of the welfare test itself.   In most families, the mother still carries the main burden of looking after the children, is better able to continue doing so, and will often (depending upon their ages and personalities) have formed a closer relationship with them.   If this is not the case, the fact that she gave birth to them may well be thought insufficient to justify giving her any preferential claim.

---

41   See para. 6.2 and paras. 2.2 and 2.5 above.

6.15   An alternative solution might be to enable the court to consider the welfare, not only of the individual child concerned, but also of each member of the family.   This is not the same as requiring the court to consider the "welfare of the family":   such a criterion could increase the risk of children being used as weapons in the matrimonial battle between their parents,[42] and would be, we consider, as retrograde a step as a return to any automatic preference between the parents. Rather, the court could be asked to consider the impact of any possible decision upon both of the parents and upon the other children in the family.

6.16   We see the merit of this as far as the other children of the family are concerned, although we have found no case in which the court was expressly faced with the dilemma of promoting the interests of one child at the expense of those of another.   Usually the courts have treated the children's interests as interdependent rather than mutually exclusive.[43]   Nevertheless, whereas a child's interests may be paramount over those of all adults, there can be no justification for making the interests of one child paramount over those of any other.   This may already be the position, as a child's upbringing may be "in question" even if he is not the subject of the particular dispute before the court.

6.17   Where the adults' interests are concerned, moreover, the case against diluting the paramountcy rule is strong.   It provides an important statement of principle, modification of which could put at risk the welfare of children.   The indications are that the paramountcy of the child's welfare needs to be strengthened and supported rather than

---

42   See e.g. Re L. [1962] 1 W.L.R. 886.

43   E.g. Adams v. Adams [1984] F.L.R. 768;   for a case where children were split see Re O. [1962] 1 W.L.R. 724.

replaced.[44] Any other approach would run counter to the whole trend of modern development in this country and elsewhere.

6.18 A further largely theoretical problem arises if the court is asked to rule in a dispute over a particular aspect of upbringing, such as medical treatment, schooling, or even, whom the child should be able to see. These questions most commonly are raised in wardship, although they may also arise following divorce or wherever persons hold parental powers jointly. Such decisions are usually made by the parent with whom the child lives. Unless a parent is also required to regard the child's welfare as paramount, which is not clear at present,[45] the court, in reaching its decision, will apply a standard different from that which the parent would be expected to follow in putting that decision into effect. It might, therefore, be suggested that a different criterion should apply to questions of "management" as opposed to custody. One possibility would be to require both court and parents merely to give "first" consideration to the child's welfare, as is the case with local authorities.[46] Another would be to permit the court to review such parental decisions only if they were outside the bounds of those which a reasonable parent might take.[47]

6.19 There are, however, serious objections to such an approach. It would be difficult to define which decisions are "managerial" and which

---

44   Law Com. No. 118 (op. cit. at n. 18), paras. 7.22-24 and e.g. A Child in Trust, (1985), Chs. 2, 20 and 31.

45   See para. 3.2 above.

46   Child Care Act 1980, s. 18(1).

47   As where agreement to adoption may be dispensed with if unreasonably withheld: Re W. [1971] A.C. 682.

"custodial". Access, for example, might be regarded as either. Furthermore, there are some apparently "managerial" decisions in which it is reasonable to expect both courts and parents to regard the welfare of the child as the paramount consideration. Our law has long taken the view, for example, that a parent's duty to provide adequate medical aid for his child outweighs any religious or other scruples he may have.[48] Any other criterion could clearly put the child at risk.[49] Further, any alternative approach would leave unclear the precise weight to be given to the child's welfare and introduce a further element of uncertainty.

6.20   There may still be doubts whether the child's "best interests" should determine the issue between parents and non-parents. Respect for family life is guaranteed under the European Convention on Human Rights[50] and parents may require protection from unwarranted interference. Local authorities are not permitted compulsorily to intervene in the care of children simply because they could provide something better, but only where specific shortcomings in the home or the parents can be proved.[51] In adoption, parental agreement is required, unless it can be dispensed with on defined grounds, and the child's welfare is only the "first" rather than the "paramount" consideration.[52] In relation to custody and upbringing, however, the House of Lords decided

---

48   R. v. Senior [1899] 1 Q.B. 283.

49   E.g. Re B. [1981] 1 W.L.R. 1421, where the court overruled the parents' withholding of consent to an operation to remove a potentially fatal intestinal blockage in their Downs syndrome baby; and see Re D. [1976] Fam. 185.

50   Article 8.

51   Children and Young Persons Act 1969, s. 1(2); Child Care Act 1980, s. 3(1); see also Review of Child Care Law ("R.C.C.L.") (1985), para. 2.13 and ch. 15, where this principle is reaffirmed.

52   C.A. 1975, s. 3 [Adoption Act 1976, s. 6].

in J. v. C.[53] that there is no presumption in favour of even the "unimpeachable" natural parents of the child, although their relationship with the child will often carry great weight as they "can be capable of ministering to the total welfare of the child in a special way".[54]

6.21   Although we recognise that this is a difficult question, several arguments persuade us that the present position in English law should be maintained.   First, the child may have a much closer relationship with someone other than his "natural" parent.   The emotional and psychological bonds which develop between a child (especially a very young child) and those who are bringing him up are just as "natural" as are his genetic ties.   To give preference over such a "psychological" parent[55] to one whose interest may be based solely on a blood tie could on occasion be highly detrimental to the child.   Secondly, the analogy with intervention by local authorities is not exact.   By definition, the authority cannot be or become such a "psychological" parent.   Whereas a non-parent applicant will usually be seeking to secure the child's existing home and an established relationship, the local authority will usually be seeking to remove him from such a home in favour of an unspecified alternative.   Unlike a case between private individuals, the court is not faced with a choice between two (or more) identifiable homes.   There are also strong objections in principle to the authority of the State being used

---

53   [1970] A.C. 688.

54   Ibid., Lord MacDermott at p. 715; c.f. Lord Upjohn at p. 724, "the natural parents [they] have themselves a strong claim to have their wishes considered as normally the proper persons to have the upbringing of the child they have brought into the world."

55   Goldstein, Freud and Solnit, Beyond the Best Interests of the Child (1973) pp. 17-20.   See B.R. v. Ealing London Borough [1985] F.L.R. 999 for a discussion of the weight to be given to 'psychological' parenthood.

to impose standards upon families unless it can be shown that the children are suffering, or are likely to suffer, unacceptable harm.[56]

6.22   We conclude, therefore, that the welfare of each child in the family should continue to be the paramount consideration whenever their custody or upbringing is in question between private individuals. The welfare test itself is well able to encompass any special contribution which natural parents can make to the emotional needs of their child, in particular to his sense of identity and self-esteem, as well as the added commitment which knowledge of their parenthood may bring.[57] We have already said that the indications are that the priority given to the welfare of the child needs to be strengthened rather than undermined.[58] We could not contemplate making any recommendation which might have the effect of weakening the protection given to children under the present law.

C.   Could the operation of the welfare test be improved?

6.23   Decision-making in custody cases presents difficulties quite unlike those of ordinary adjudication.[59] Although past events are sometimes in dispute, more commonly the court is concerned to evaluate the characters and personalities of the various people involved, including

---

56   Mnookin, "Child Custody Adjudication Judicial Functions in the Face of Indeterminacy" (1975) 39 L.C.P. 226, 260-262, and R.C.C.L. (op. cit. at n. 51), para. 15.10.

57   Lord Simon of Glaisdale in Re D. [1977] A.C. 602, 638C said that "courts of matrimonial jurisdiction in general proceed nowadays, on the basis that it is in the best interests of the child to grow up to know, and if possible to respect and love, both the natural parents". See also M. v. J. [1977] 3 F.L.R. 19, Re C. (M.A.) [1966] 1 W.L.R. 646 and Re E.(P.) [1968] 1 W.L.R. 1913.

58   See para. 6.17 above.

59   Mnookin (op. cit. at n. 56), pp. 249-262.

the child. It will then have to predict how the various participants will react to one another and to future events, including the court's own decision. Above all, it must decide what outcome it wishes to secure for the child and what course will best promote it. All of these involve considerable uncertainty and often value judgments, as to which opinions may understandably differ.[60]

6.24   There are obvious risks in such a state of affairs. Although courts have repeatedly stressed that "individual cases are infinitely varied" and it is "unwise to rely upon any rule of thumb",[61] it is undeniable that "propositions"[62] akin to rules of thumb have from time to time been developed and applied. Statements that, for example, effect should be given to the "dictates of nature that the mother is the natural guardian, protector and comforter of very young children"[63] have clearly played a part in resolving not only the case in question but others too. The great majority of custody cases are uncontested, and the parties must to some extent have based their negotiations upon their own or their advisers' understanding of how such propositions might be applied.[64]

---

60   Ibid., pp. 260-262; see e.g. May v. May [1986] F.L.R. 325.

61   Pountney v. Morris [1984] F.L.R. 381, 384 per Dunn L.J.

62   Ormrod L.J. in Bowley v. Bowley [1984] F.L.R. 791 at p. 795 and see Townson v. Mahon [1984] F.L.R. 690.

63   Re K. [1977] Fam. 179, 189 per Stamp L.J.; see also Ormrod L.J. at p. 191, "I cannot imagine any court deciding to give children of 5½ and 2½ to the father when a perfectly competent mother is able to offer them, physically speaking, a perfectly satisfactory home." See also cases cited at n. 39 above.

64   Mnookin, "Bargaining in the Shadow of the Law: The Case of Divorce" (1979) C.L.P. 65. See also the Supplement to this paper, Priest and Whybrow, Custody Law in Practice in the Divorce and Domestic Courts (1986).

6.25   The advantage of such informal propositions is that they may be developed in line with current developments in professional as well as public opinion.[65]   They need not remain fixed in the understanding or values of a previous age. The disadvantage is that they may not, in fact, represent the standards of the community as a whole or of the particular families involved, but only of a certain section. They have never been subject to Parliamentary scrutiny and if they were might well prove controversial.   Their nature, content and effect remains uncertain, because, in theory, they are no more than common sense obsevations, usually to be applied "when all else is equal".[66]

6.26   On the other hand, without such propositions, there is an obvious risk that, given the large number of cases and the many different courts in which they may be heard,[67] essentially the same sort of case will be approached in a very different way, or according to very different standards or values, from court to court. As it is, although the appellate courts have attempted to guide lower courts in the application of section 1, their role is inevitably limited by the recognition that each case is different, precedents are generally unhelpful,[68] and all generalisations must be qualified.[69]

---

65   Contrast Re Thain [1926] Ch 676, with J. v. C. [1970] A.C. 668. Lord MacDermott in the latter case, at p. 715, stressed that Eve J.'s opinion expressed in Re Thain that a change of custody for a young child would result in merely transient upset has been superseded by "growing experience ... that serious harm even to young children may, on occasion, be caused."

66   B. v. B. [1985] F.L.R. 166, 182 per Oliver L.J.

67   See Part I, n. 6.

68   Re K. [1977] Fam. 179, 183 per Stamp L.J.

69   Re W. (1982) 4 F.L.R. 492, 504 per Cumming-Bruce L.J.

6.27   In attempting to solve or at least to reduce some of the difficulties, there are two main approaches which might be considered and have indeed been adopted in some other jurisdictions:

> (i)   a set of statutory objectives, or guidelines, interpreting what constitutes a child's best interests; or

> (ii)   a statutory checklist or a list of factors which the court should be obliged to consider.

Although these two approaches may result in similar statutory expressions, they can be distinguished in principle. The former sets out substantive or prescriptive rules which will guide the courts' decision. The latter lays down matters to which consideration should be given in the process of reaching a decision.

(i)   Guidelines

6.28   It could be argued that, as in several American States,[70] Parliament should decide upon and set down clearly the direction in which it is desired that the courts should go. At their most firm, guidelines could become rules of law, as, for example, in some Latin American countries.[71] Less firm guidelines could operate as presumptions, which

---

70   Alabama, California, Georgia, Kansas, Louisiana, and Texas.

71   Where the courts may rely on fixed rules. In some countries custody is awarded to the 'innocent' spouse following a 'fault' divorce (e.g. Brazil and Venezeula). In Bolivia if the parties cannot agree, custody is decided on the basis of either custody of girls being granted to their mothers, and boys to their fathers, or on the basis of custody of children under 7 being granted to their mothers and those over 7 to their fathers. In Argentina custody of children under 5 is given to the mother; otherwise custody is given to the party best able to provide for education.

would determine the outcome unless they could be rebutted on the facts of each case: as, for example, in those of the United States which have provided for joint custody[72] or for a preference in favour of natural parents.[73]

6.29   Such guidelines might well provide relative certainty and consistency of outcome.   Hence they could reduce stressful litigation, which is "deeply damaging to the parents and their relationship, rubbing off generally in damage to the children involved".[74]   Guidelines might also encourage the parties and courts to reach final decisions, rather than tentative solutions which may require reconsideration later.   In Australia, for example, the court is directed to make the order which is least likely to lead to the institution of further proceedings.[75]

6.30   Two difficulties, however, are framing acceptable guidelines and the fact that the guidelines may conflict in a given case.   In Part III of this paper, we tentatively proposed seven "yardsticks" against which to judge proposed reforms in the law, not only in the resolution of contested cases but also in the design of the system as a whole.[76]   With a little adaptation, those yardsticks might be turned into guidelines of the sort under discussion here.   We would very much welcome views as to whether they might prove acceptable and what modifications could be proposed.

---

72   E.g. California, Florida, Kansas, Louisiana, and Nevada.

73   California, Georgia, Kansas, Louisiana, Oregon (in favour of the family home) and Texas.

74   B. v. B. [1985] F.L.R. 166, 185 per Cumming-Bruce L.J.

75   Family Law Act 1975, s. 64(1)(ba), as amended by the Family Law Amendment Act 1983.

76   See paras. 3.7-3.8.

6.31 The main problem with guidelines, however, is that it is difficult to frame them in such a way that they do not undermine the paramountcy rule itself. This is well illustrated by the three guidelines which have been suggested as being the only ones which can be justified by the prevailing state of knowledge about the needs of children:[77]

(i) not putting the child at risk of harm,

(ii) preferring a "psychological" parent over any other claimant, and

(iii) subject to the two previous rules, preferring the natural parents.

There are also obvious difficulties in defining what constitutes "psychological parenthood" and "fitness" for this purpose. Furthermore, such guidelines would not assist a court in resolving that most typical of disputes, between two parents to whom the child is equally attached, who are equally committed to him, and who can provide equally good homes for him.

6.32 In our view, the only guidelines which could be developed to resolve such cases would have potentially arbitrary and undesirable results, and place the party against whom they run at an unfair disadvantage. It is known, for example, that the courts are usually reluctant to disturb the child's existing home,[78] even where the other parent may have had at least as good a relationship with the child and

---

77 Mnookin (op. cit. at n. 56), pp. 282-287.

78 Re C. (1980) 2 F.L.R. 163; B. v. B. [1985] F.L.R. 166.

have an equally satisfactory alternative home to offer. Any guideline to that effect, however, would be advantageous to a parent who was able to delay proceedings or a parent who had made life intolerable and caused the other to leave and give up care of the child during the interim period. On the other hand, preferences based upon the sex of the parent or of the child, although they still exist in other jurisdictions, are unlikely to prove acceptable here. They "have been tried historically and are now being discarded ... because they reflect value judgments and sexual stereotypes that our society is in the process of rejecting".[79]

6.33   These considerations lead us to conclude that each case should continue to be approached without any proposition in favour of a particular result. Section 1 itself adds that the court shall not take into account "from any other point of view" than the child's welfare whether the claim of either parent is superior to that of the other. In New Zealand and in several of the United States, the legislature has gone further, to provide that "there shall be no presumption that the placing of a child in the custody of a particular person will, because of the sex of that person, best serve the welfare of the child".[80]   A further provision which is found in New Zealand and some American statutes[81] is that the court shall have regard to the conduct of any parent only insofar as it is relevant to the welfare of the child.   Although we doubt whether

---

79   Mnookin (op. cit. at n. 56), p. 284.

80   New Zealand Guardianship Act 1968, s. 23(1A).   It has been said that this "appears ... to be superfluous window-dressing inserted to placate dissident and obstinate elements who considered themselves unable to accept the law as it was being administered previously": Webb, Family Law 1986 Style (1986), p. 138.   In North America, see e.g. Arizona, California, Colorado, Florida and Kentucky.

81   E.g. in the States of Colorado, Kentucky, Oregon, South Dakota, and the Virgin Islands.

these are strictly necessary,[82] we invite views as to whether such specific provisions would counteract the tendency towards sub-rules which undoubtedly exists at present.

(ii)   Checklist

6.34   A checklist of matters for the court to take into account is a common means in other jurisdictions of assisting the court in operating the welfare principle. Some of these may be more akin to guidelines and thus open to the criticisms mentioned above. More usually, however, a checklist recites the relevant factors to be taken into consideration, as does section 25(2) of the Matrimonial Causes Act 1973 in relation to financial provision and property adjustment after divorce, without indicating the result to be achieved. An example of a recently enacted checklist is found in the Australian Family Law Act 1975, as amended by the Family Law Amendment Act 1983. Section 64(1)(bb) provides that the court shall take the following matters into account:

(i)   the nature of the relationship of the child with each of the parents of the child and with other persons;

(ii)   the effect on the child of any separation from -

(A)   either parent of the child; or

(B)   any child, or other person, with whom the child has been living;

(iii)   the desirability of, and the effect of, any change in the existing arrangements for the care of the child;

(iv)   the attitude to the child, and to the responsibilities and duties of parenthood, demonstrated by each parent of the child;

---

82   Since J. v. C. [1970] A.C. 688 the meaning of the paramountcy principle has been clear. See para. 6.9 above.

(v)   the capacity of each parent or of any other person, to provide adequately for the needs of the child, including the emotional and intellectual needs of the child;

(vi)   any other fact or circumstance (including the education and upbringing of the child) that, in the opinion of the court, the welfare of the child requires to be taken into account.

A checklist may be used in addition to guidelines. As we have already mentioned, the Family Law Act combines this list with a general objective of making the order which is "least likely to lead to the institution of further proceedings" with respect to the child.[83]

6.35   Checklists are found in nearly all the Canadian Provinces and several American States. There are clear advantages in establishing a non-exhaustive set of relevant factors which in no way hampers the development of substantive case law or risks creating a bias in favour of certain parties. It simply aims to ensure that all the relevant considerations are taken fully into account and also, perhaps, to provide some consistency from court to court and case to case.

6.36   The existing lists differ considerably in both content and style. In Canada, for example, there are seven Provinces[84] with long lists of factors to be taken into account in determining the best interests of the child but the only factor common to all is the views and preferences of the child, to the extent that these can be ascertained. All of the lists also refer to the mental, emotional and physical needs of the child, but not in exactly the same terms. Most of them refer to the quality of the child's existing relationships with parents, brothers and sisters, and others;

---

83   Family Law Act 1975 s. 64(1)(ba), as amended by the Family Law Amendment Act 1983.

84   British Columbia, Manitoba, New Brunswick, Newfoundland, Ontario, Prince Edward Island and Saskatchewan (including checklists used in child welfare legislation).

to the capacity of each party to discharge the obligations of a parent and sometimes to their future plans; and to the ability of the child to achieve his full potential in the home proposed. Somewhat surprisingly, the effect upon the child of disruption in his existing home appears in only three of the lists and the security or stability of the future home in only two. His cultural and religious background features in three, and provision for his "spiritual well-being" in another. Other factors mentioned include relationship by blood or adoption and the effect on the child of any delay in a final order.

6.37 Possible disadvantages of such lists are that they could not hope to be definitive and it may be misleading to highlight certain matters to the exclusion of others. Further, the wording may inevitably be general and thus not of any great assistance. Despite the differences in style, however, there is sufficient common ground between those which we have mentioned to suggest that an acceptable checklist could be devised here were it thought helpful to do so.

6.38 On the basis of the current approach of the English courts, we suggest that the court might be required to take into account all the relevant circumstances in assessing the child's welfare, including the following:

(1) the quality of the love, affection and other emotional ties existing between the child and each of the parties;[85]

---

85 For a recent example see Stephenson v. Stephenson [1985] F.L.R. 1140, 1148, where there was a "lack of true bonding between this mother and the child" (per Wood J.).

(2)   the nature of the emotional ties existing between the child and any person other than the parties;[86]

(3)   the effect upon the child of separation from either party or from any other person with whom he has been living;[87]

(4)   the capacity and disposition of each of the parties to provide for the child's emotional needs in the future,[88] including the recognition of his ties with other people;[89]

(5)   the length of time the child has lived in his existing environment and the effect of any change, including changes of neighbourhood, school, local activities and access to relatives and friends;[90]

---

86   E.g. an extended family and "a perfectly splendid stepmother-to-be": Stephenson v. Stephenson (ibid.), pp. 1146 and 1147.

87   "Where ... a child of 2 years of age has been brought up without interruption by the mother (or a mother substitute) it should not be removed from her care unless there are strong counterveiling reasons for doing so" D. v. M. [1983] Fam. 33, 41 per Ormrod L.J. See also J. v. C. [1970] A.C. 668 and B.R. v. Ealing London Borough [1985] F.L.R. 999.   C.f. where the continuity of care has been broken: Re C. (1980) 2 F.L.R. 163.

88   The "capacity of the grown-ups who are put forward as claimants for care and control is of immense importance in proving their capacity for forming affectionate, loving relationships with the child ..." Re W. (1982) 4 F.L.R. 492, 504, per Cumming-Bruce L.J. As to a child's need to know his natural parents, see n. 57.

89   The willingness of one parent to provide the child's access to the other is an important consideration: D. v. M. [1983] Fam. 33, 41. In some North American states, for example California, an express preference is given to such a 'friendly' parent.

90   "She has been able to put down roots and to form happy relationships with all those about her": Stephenson v. Stephenson (op. cit. at n. 85), p. 1146 per Wood J.

(6)   the capacity (bearing in mind any financial provision or
        property adjustment which may be ordered) and
        disposition of each of the parties to provide properly for
        the child's accommodation,[91] hygiene, food, medical
        care, appropriate supervision[92] and companionship and
        otherwise for his physical needs and development;[93]

(7)   the capacity (bearing in mind any financial provision
        which may be ordered) and disposition of each of the
        parties to provide properly for the child's education and
        intellectual development both at home and at school;[94]

(8)   the capacity and disposition of each of the parties to
        provide properly for the child's social and ethical
        development;[95]

(9)   where relevant, the ethnic, cultural or religious[96]
        background of the child and each of the parties;[97]

---

91   Re F. [1969] 2 Ch. 238, 243 but in most cases "disadvantages of a
        material sort must be of little weight": Stephenson v. Stephenson
        (ibid.), p. 1148.

92   For a child to have his time divided between 3 or 4 adults including
        a child-minder and relatives is to be avoided if possible: D. v. M.
        [1983] Fam. 33, 41.   See also Re K. [1977] Fam. 179.

93   For an example of a general discussion of a parent's capacity and
        disposition, see Re B.A. [1985] F.L.R. 1008;   as to medical care see
        Jane v. Jane (1983) 4 F.L.R. 712.

94   May v. May [1986] F.L.R. 325.

95   C.f. e.g. S. v. S. (1978) 1 F.L.R. 143;   Re P. (1982) 4 F.L.R. 401;   Re
        B. and G. [1985] F.L.R. 493.

96   Re M. [1967] 3 All E.R. 1071, Re C. (MA) [1966] 1 W.L.R. 646;   Re
        T. (1975) 2 F.L.R. 239 and Wright v. Wright (1980) 2 F.L.R. 276.

97   Jussa v. Jussa [1972] 1 W.L.R. 881, Haleem v. Haleem (1975) 5 Fam.
        Law 184.

(10)   the quality of the relationship existing or likely to exist between the child and any other member of each household and the likely effect of that member upon the capacities and dispositions of each of the parties in paragraphs (4), (6), (7) and (8) above;[98]

(11)   any risk of ill-treatment by either party or by any present or likely member of that party's household;[99]

(12)   any other special circumstances, including any particular aptitude or disability of the child;

(13)   the wishes and feelings of the child.[100]

6.39   Such a checklist is designed for cases where the allocation of guardianship or care and control is in question.   Nevertheless, it could be used for the determination of more precise issues of upbringing even if some factors would play little part in many cases.   Our provisional conclusion is that, while guidelines should not be adopted, a checklist of relevant factors might be helpful.   We welcome views upon the general question and upon the list which we have tentatively proposed.

D.   The wishes and feelings of the child

6.40   One relevant factor which is common to all the checklists we have found and is often prescribed in countries which have no such lists is the views of the child himself.   In adoption cases, the court is required to

---

98   For the benefits of a stable step-family, see Stephenson v. Stephenson [1985] F.L.R. 1140, Re C. (1980) 2 F.L.R. 163 and Re D.W. (1983) 14 Fam. Law 17.

99   E.g. L. v. L. (1980) 2 F.L.R. 48, where the father was alleged to have over-severely chastised the child.

100   See paras. 6.40-6.44 below.

ascertain the "wishes and feelings" of the child so far as this is practicable, and give due consideration to them "having regard to his age and understanding".[101] There is no such requirement in custody law. However, the court will rarely, if ever, make a custody order which is contrary to the wishes of a child who has reached 16.[102] Below that age, his views may be taken into account but will be treated with some caution;[103] nor should the child be placed in the invidious position of having to choose between his parents.[104]

6.41 There is clearly a strong case for including the adoption formula in custody cases. By referring to the child's "feelings", it allows his views to be sought indirectly, without subjecting him to any pressure to choose between his parents, or between his parents and others. At the same time, it recognises that the child, not the adult parties, is the central person in the case and entitled to consideration in his own right.

6.42 This point has been reinforced by the decision of the House of Lords in Gillick v. West Norfolk and Wisbech Area Health Authority.[105]

---

101 C.A. 1975, s. 3 [Adoption Act 1976, s. 6].

102 Hall v. Hall [1946] 175 L.T. 355. In New Zealand a custody order shall not be made in respect of a 16 year old unless there are special circumstances: s. 24(1), Guardianship Act 1968. A custody order made under that age expires once a child reaches 16 unless the court has otherwise ordered "in special circumstances": s. 24(2) of the 1968 Act. Custody in New Zealand means the right to care of the child: s. 3 of the 1968 Act.

103 D. v. D. [1958] C.L.Y. 981 Re S. [1967] 1 W.L.R. 396; Guery v. Guery [1982] 12 Fam. Law 184; Re D.W. (1983) 14 Fam. Law 17.

104 Adams v. Adams [1984] F.L.R. 768. The Australian Family Law Act 1975 imposed a duty to consider the child's wishes but has recently been amended to clarify that the child may not be compelled to express a view (ss. 64(1)(b) and (1A)).

105 [1986] A.C. 112.

Indeed, it could be argued that, just as the parent's power to decide what medical treatment his child should have gives way to the child's right to make that decision for himself once he is competent to do so, so also does the parent's power to decide where the child should live.[106] If so, an order for custody or care and control might be ineffective against an older child, unless it was made clear that the court could insist where the parents could not. As such, the order would impinge upon the child's own rights, and the case for recognising his wishes as an independent consideration alongside his welfare would become even stronger.

6.43   Any such change in the substantive law inevitably raises the questions of when and how the child's own views should be put before the court. There would have to be some means of doing so independently of the case presented by the adult parties. In adoption and custodianship there is invariably a report, either from a guardian ad litem or from the adoption agency or from the local authority, in which this can be done.[107] In other custody cases, there is usually a welfare officers' report if the issue is contested, and it is normal practice to interview the child, although officers differ as to the minimum age at which this can be attempted.[108] The judge (but not a magistrates' court) may interview the child in private. In uncontested cases, however, welfare officers'

---

106   See Eekelaar, "Gillick in the Divorce Court" (1986) 136 N.L.J. 184. Children should be consulted, if their degree of maturity permits, when the court takes a decision "relating to the attribution or exercise of parental responsibilities and affecting (their) essential interests", Principle 3 of Parental Responsibilities, Recommendation, No. R(84)4 adopted by the Committee of Ministers of the Council of Europe on 28 February 1984.

107   As to adoption see C.A. 1975, s. 18 and the Adoption Rules 1984, rr. 18 and 22. As to custodianship see paras. 2.80-2.82.

108   See Eekelaar, "Children in Divorce: Some Further Data" (1982) 2 O.J.L.S. 63, 84.

reports are relatively rare, as is the child's attendance at the section 41 appointment. Requiring the court to canvass the child's wishes and feelings in every case would entail a considerable change from current practice and, given the numbers involved,[109] a considerable increase in costs. Such procedural questions are outside the scope of this paper, but we invite views as to whether the substantive law might be modified to take account of the practical difficulties in uncontested cases.

6.44   Similarly, the issue of how the child's point of view can best be ascertained and represented to the court is subsidiary to the question of whether the substantive law should require this to be done. The choice between the various methods outlined in Part II is a difficult one and we do not intend to rehearse the arguments here. For the time being, our provisional view is that the court in custody cases should be required to ascertain and consider the wishes and feelings of the child concerned. We would welcome views as to whether this should be made an independent provision in its own right, or simply appear as part of the checklist suggested earlier.

---

109   See para. 4.1 above.

PART VII

CONCLUSION

7.1   We conclude by pulling together some of the proposals made in this paper and in our earlier paper on Guardianship[1] in order to give an outline of a possible new scheme for the allocation of parental responsibilities and to discuss the statutory form which it might take. Our aims[2] are to eliminate the present gaps, inconsistencies and anomalies; to produce a simple system which can be readily understood by the people involved; and above all to promote the interests of the children concerned in accordance with the objectives which we put forward in Part III.   We should emphasise that these are only tentative proposals and that on each point other options are canvassed in the paper. These are summarised before the new scheme is outlined.

A.   Summary of the options

7.2   We begin by examining, in the light of the available research evidence and other material, the arguments for and against the divorce courts' present duty to approve the arrangements proposed for the children of the family.[3]   The procedure has not been noticeably successful in achieving any of its original aims and we discuss four possible options for reform:[4]

---

1   Working Paper No. 91 (1985).

2   See paras. 1.2, 1.3 and 3.7.

3   Paras. 4.8 to 4.10.

4   Para. 4.11.

(i)   abolition;

(ii)   improving the procedure;

(iii)   strengthening both substance and procedure;

(iv)   modifying the substance so as to reflect more modest aims.

7.3   We provisionally conclude, as did the Booth Committee, that this provision cannot be abolished without putting something in its place, because it stresses the need to give special attention to the children whose homes are breaking up and nothing should be done to detract from this.[5] The Booth Committee's recommendations should make the procedure more effective in discovering the parties' proposals and directing appropriate services and conciliation towards those families who could benefit from them.   These improvements should reinforce the responsibility of the parents themselves.[6]   That responsibility could, however, be undermined by the courts' present duty to be satisfied with their arrangements, when in most cases there is little alternative.

7.4   Hence we suggest a modified formula which would enable the court to consider the information put before it but with a view to discovering whether there is a _prima facie_ case for an order and, if so, which, rather than deciding that the arrangements are "satisfactory" or "the best that can be devised in the circumstances".[7]   We also examine the arguments for and against making any order in those divorce cases

---

5   Para. 4.12.

6   Para. 4.13.

7   Para. 4.15-4.16.

where the parties are on relatively amicable terms and wish to continue to co-operate over their children's future. We conclude that a flexible approach is likely to be most helpful.[8] It is not always necessary to make an order to sanction the parents' arrangements and they should remain free to modify them by agreement.[9] There will still be cases, no doubt the majority, where a court order is needed to give security and stability to child and parents alike.

7.5 We then examine the merits and demerits of the orders commonly made between parents, for sole custody to one with reasonable access to the other,[10] or for joint custody[11] with care and control to one and reasonable access to the other, and other possible orders under the present system.[12] The present law is confusing, uncertain and unnecessarily restrictive. There appear to be three options for reform:[13]

(i)   to leave the court to allocate parental responsibilities as it sees fit;[14]

(ii)   to clarify and harmonise the effects of the present orders;[15] and

---

8   Para. 4.21.

9   Para. 4.59(v).

10   Paras. 4.23 to 4.26.

11   Paras. 4.35 to 4.43.

12   Paras. 4.44 to 4.46.

13   Para. 4.47.

14   Para. 4.48.

15   Paras. 4.49 to 4.50.

(iii)   to attempt a new approach, in which parents retain their equal parental status and share their child's time between them.[16]

7.6   As it appears to us that parents have responsibilities rather than rights and that children often benefit from a real rather than a largely symbolic sharing of those responsibilities we tentatively favour the third of these options, which could be applied to all the jurisdictions in which custody is allocated between parents. As it forms the core of our new scheme we shall explain it further below.

7.7   At present, three categories of people may be granted custody of children who are not their own: spouses who have treated the child as a member of their family, people qualified to apply for custodianship, and third parties who intervene or are identified by the court in matrimonial or custody proceedings begun by others.[17] Each of these categories has been developed in a different context and for a different reason. The result is a system with no consistent theme or guiding principle in which it can be a matter of chance whether a non-parent can be granted custody.[18] This is particularly apparent in the case of step-parents, whose position differs according to whether the natural parents were unmarried, or divorced or one of them has died, and according to whether the step-parent's own marriage to the parent has broken down.

7.8   We canvass three possible approaches to defining the people who may apply for or be granted custody:

---

16   Para. 4.51 to 4.57.

17   Para. 5.2.

18   Para. 5.29.

(i)   allowing any person to apply for custody of a "child of the family" without having to apply for matrimonial relief; the concept could be extended beyond married couples and thus replace the present qualifications for custodianship;[19]

(ii)   modifying the residential and consent requirements for custodianship so as to approximate more closely to the recommendations of the Houghton Committee which proposed the procedure;[20]

(iii)   allowing non-parents the same rights to apply for custody as parents have, perhaps with leave of the court.[21]

7.9   It would not be possible to remove or curtail the present rights of spouses in relation to children of the family, so that it would be difficult to achieve a consistent and simplified system while their position co-exists with the custodianship regime. There seems, however, little reason why non-parents should not have the same rights to apply as have parents, subject perhaps to the need to obtain the leave of the court. This is already possible in a large number of cases and there is little reason to suppose that it would expose the child or his parents to the risks of unwarranted claims. In practice most who might wish to apply to assume full-time responsibility for a child will already have a close relationship with him. We conclude, therefore, that provided that unwarranted claims

---

19   Paras. 5.30 to 5.33.

20   Paras. 5.34 to 5.36.   For the Houghton Committee's recommendations see paras. 5.15 to 5.18.

21   Paras. 5.37 to 5.40.

can be excluded artificial barriers should not be errected against securing the outcome which will be best for the child.[22]

7.10   The same considerations cannot apply to access or to other more limited questions of upbringing.   Access is a less onerous responsibility than custody and a completely "open door" could subject parents and children to claims from "interfering busybodies". We think, therefore, that applications for access should be restricted to people who are likely to have been important to the child. We do, however, suggest that the present categories (rather different from those who can apply for or be granted custody) could be rationalised and extended.[23]

7.11   Nor do the same considerations apply to children in local authority care,[24] where the arguments in favour of open access must be balanced against the need to maintain the willingness of parents to use the voluntary child care system, particularly if it is to be extended to other categories of children in the future, and also against the need to strengthen rather than to undermine the responsibilities of local authorities themselves to make the best provision and plan the best future for their children, particularly those in compulsory care. We conclude, therefore, that some restriction is necessary in the case of children in care.[25]

7.12   Once again, there are three possible options as to the orders available:[26]

---

22   Ibid., and para. 5.63(i).

23   Paras. 5.57 and 5.60; for details see para. 7.33 below.

24   Paras. 5.41 to 5.48.

25   Para. 5.48; for details see para. 7.34 below.

26   Para. 5.53.

(i)   to leave the court to allocate parental responsibilities as it sees fit;[27]

(ii)   to clarify and harmonise the effects of the present orders;[28] or

(iii)   a new approach to complement that for parents, whereby non-parents would usually be appointed guardians, sharing care and control with one another or with parents as appropriate.[29]

Once again, we tentatively favour the new approach, which we explain in more detail below.

7.13   Finally, we discuss the rule that, in any proceedings where the custody or upbringing of a child is in question, his welfare shall be the first and paramount consideration.   There are various arguments for modifying the paramountcy rule, but the indications are that it needs to be strengthened rather than the reverse.   It is an important statement of the principle that adults are expected to put the children's welfare before their own and any modification could put the welfare of children seriously at risk.[30]

---

27   Para. 5.54.

28   Paras. 5.55-5.56.

29   Paras. 5.57 to 5.60.

30   Para. 6.22.

7.14　　　There is, however, some risk of inconsistency and subjectivity in applying the welfare test[31] and other countries have sought to mitigate this by laying down statutory guidelines as to what will be of benefit to a child.　We consider, however, that such guidelines would be inaccurate, arbitrary or unfair, and could undermine the paramountcy rule itself.[32] On the other hand, a "checklist" of factors to be taken into account in assessing the child's welfare has proved helpful in other jurisdictions and might also be adopted here.[33]　　Whether or not such a checklist is adopted, a factor which should always be considered is the wishes and feelings of the child himself to the extent that this is appropriate in view of his age and understanding.[34]

B.　　An outline of the possible new scheme

Parenthood

7.15　　　Parenthood would become the primary legal concept in the allocation of responsibility for bringing up a child.[35]　　Parents[36] who are

---

31　　Para. 6.26.

32　　Para. 6.31 and 6.33.

33　　Paras. 6.34 to 6.39; for details see para. 7.38 below.

34　　Paras. 6.40 to 6.44.

35　　See Working Paper No. 91, para. 3.4.

36　　At present "parent" usually means the man whose sperm or the woman whose ovum contributed to the embryo formed; in our Report on Illegitimacy (1982) Law Com. No. 118, para. 12.9, we have recommended that a child conceived by A.I.D. with the consent of the mother's husband should be treated in law as her husband's child; a _fortiori_ the woman in whom is implanted the ovum of another, fertilised elsewhere, should be treated in law as the child's mother; this probably requires no legislation, but could be clarified.

married to one another when or after the child is conceived should continue to have equal responsibilities. Others, including a father who is not married to the mother at or after the child's conception,[37] would only acquire such responsibility through guardianship or court order.

7.16   Parenthood would entail a primary claim and a primary responsibility to bring up the child.   It would not, however, entail parental "rights" as such.   The House of Lords, in <u>Gillick</u> v. <u>West Norfolk and Wisbech Area Health Authority</u>,[38] has held that the powers which parents have to control or make decisions for their children are simply to the necessary concomitant of their parental duties.   This confirms our view that "to talk of parental 'rights' is not only inaccurate as a matter of juristic analysis but also a misleading use of ordinary language".[39]   We suggest, therefore, that the expression should no longer be used in legislation.

7.17   A further consequence of this, we also suggest,[40] is that the exercise of most parental responsibilities cannot be separated from the care and control of the child.   The actual care of the child will carry with it the responsibility to look after him and to bring him up and it will also carry the power to control him in order to do this properly.   Hence, in our proposed new scheme of orders, parental powers and parental responsibilities are not opposites but go hand in hand.   For the most part,

---

37   This would confirm the policy recommended in Law Com. No. 118 (ibid.), and cl. 34 of the draft Family Law Reform Bill annexed.

38   [1986] A.C. 112.

39   Law Com. No. 118, para. 4.18; Working Paper No. 91, para. 1.11.

40   See paras. 4.51 to 4.53.

they also "run with the child". We do not believe it to be either practicable or in the interests of children for those who are looking after them to be unable to do what they believe to be best for the child at the time that it has to be done.

7.18   In most families, of course, the parents are living together and able to share these responsibilities between them.   Once a relationship has been established between parent and child, we believe that the law should disturb it as little as possible.   Hence unless and until a court orders otherwise, parents will have equal responsibilities and will be able to exercise them independently of one another.[41]   They will also remain free to agree between themselves as to the exercise of any of their responsibilities, although this would not be enforced if it were not for the child's benefit to do so.[42]

7.19   There are some families who can continue to operate in this way even though the adults are separated for all or most of the time. There should be no assumption that it is necessary to reallocate parental responsibilities by court order simply because there are other proceedings between the parents.   The court should have a discretion as to whether or not to make orders, depending upon the circumstances of the case.   The security of the child, and of the parent with whom he will be spending most of his time, should, however, be important factors in that decision.[43]

---

41   See paras. 2.2 and 4.57.

42   Paras. 2.3 and 4.59(v).

43   Para. 4.21.

The duty of the court

7.20   In specified matrimonial proceedings, the parties should be under a duty to furnish particulars to the court as to the present and future upbringing of the children.   The court should be under a duty not to conclude the proceedings between the adults until it has decided what order, if any, should be made about the children.   These duties should apply in divorce, nullity and judicial separation proceedings under the Matrimonial Causes Act 1973 and in proceedings for financial relief under that Act and under the Domestic Proceedings and Magistrates' Courts Act 1978.[44]

7.21   We invite views as to whether they should also apply in proceedings for personal protection orders under that Act, or for injunctions under section 1 of the Domestic Violence and Matrimonial Proceedings Act 1976, or for orders under the Matrimonial Homes Act 1983.[45]   If they are to be applied to proceedings under the 1976 Act it would be necessary to extend them from "children of the family" to children "living with" the applicant.[46]   In any event, the duty could be confined to children under 16.[47]

The powers of the court

7.22   The court should have power to make orders in respect of the upbringing of children, of its own motion or upon application in the course of any relevant proceedings, irrespective of the outcome of the case

---

44   Para. 4.16.

45   See paras. 2.9 and 2.10.

46   This expression is used in sections 1 and 2 of the 1976 Act, presumably because they cover unmarried couples, to whom the expression "child of the family" cannot at present apply.

47   See para. 4.16.

between the adult parties. Relevant proceedings would include all the matrimonial proceedings referred to above as well as applications to resolve any question relating to parental responsibilities. The orders available would be as follows:

(i) Guardianship

7.23 A guardianship order would be used to confer parental responsibility upon a non-parent acting in loco parentis.[48] It would replace the present powers to confer custody or legal custody upon step-parents, custodians and unmarried fathers, as well as the proposed power to confer parental rights and duties upon unmarried fathers.[49] It would enable a step-parent or unmarried father to share parental responsibility with a parent. It would normally comprise all the responsibilities of a parent, but exceptions or restrictions could be specified in the order. "Guardianship" is preferred to "custodianship", not only because we see no reason why responsibility for any property the child may have should automatically be excluded,[50] but also because it emphasises our view that the status involves commitment to and responsibility for the child rather than entitlement.

(ii) Care and control

7.24 A care and control order could be used to allocate the child's time between people with parenthood or guardianship.[51] Most commonly, this would be between parents following divorce or separation,

---

48 Working Paper No. 91, para. 4.38 and para. 5.58 above.

49 Law Com. No. 118 (op. cit. at n. 36), paras. 7.26 to 7.33.

50 For the uncertain state of the law relating to the powers of parents and guardians in this respect, see Working Paper No. 91, paras. 2.32 to 2.34.

51 See paras. 4.51 et seq. above.

but it could also apply between guardians, or between parent and guardian. It would replace the present powers to award custody, legal custody, actual custody and access as between these people.

7.25 Care and control would be capable of being shared even where the parents or guardians were living in different households, but in such cases the court would probably make no order at all. Where an order is required care and control would be allocated by time. Both parents would retain their parental status but parental responsibilities would largely "run with the child": the parent with care and control would thus be able and obliged to exercise those responsibilities while the child was with him.

7.26 The court would have power to signify for what periods of time or in what manner care and control should be shared. It would also be able to attach conditions, specifying matters in respect of which one or other parent was not to have the power of independent action.[52] Change of name, leaving the country, adoption and marriage would continue to be dealt with specifically by statute or rules of court.

7.27 Care and control could often be allocated between parents on the basis of their continuing equal status, even though one might have the child for a much greater proportion of time than the other. The other parent would not be able to restrict or interfere in the exercise of parental responsibility by the parent who had the child, unless this was provided for in the order, but would retain his parental status with respect to third parties, so that for example he could ask for school reports and other information. The same would apply in reverse while the child was with him, so that his status and responsibility as a parent would be clearly recognised during what is currently called access.

---

52 See paras. 4.54 to 4.56 for examples and discussion.

7.28   However, the allocation could be such that one parent had only very limited time with the child and was restricted in what he could do while the child was with him.[53]   Thus it would still be possible to limit one parent's role to the equivalent of access under the present law.   If our analysis of parenthood is right, there is no need to go further in securing the position of the parent who is carrying the main burden of responsibility for the child.   We invite views, however, as to whether the court should additionally have power to confer sole guardianship upon one parent, thus divesting the other of almost all responsibility for the child.[54]

7.29   The same considerations would apply as between parents and non-parent guardians.   The appointment of a guardian with care and control for most of the child's time would not deprive the parent of his status but for most of the time the guardian would be exercising parental responsibilities.   Particular restrictions could, however, be tailored to the individual case, where for example the child had an established religious faith or was being educated in a particular way.

(iii) Visiting

7.30   Visiting orders would be used where the visitor was not the child's parent or guardian but a grandparent or other person who might at present be awarded access.[55]   Such a person would have the responsibility, which anyone has, to protect and care for the child while the child is with him but would not be able to take any step which would interfere with the child's usual way of life.   The same would apply to parents if it were thought necessary to retain a power to deprive them of parental powers and responsibilities in some cases.

---

53   See paras. 4.57 and 4.59.

54   See Working Paper No. 91, paras. 4.36 and 4.37.

55   Para. 5.61-5.62.

(iv) Particular questions

7.31   Finally the court would have a general power to resolve any particular question relating to the upbringing of a child arising between parents or guardians.

Who may apply?

7.32   For the reasons already explained, parents would be able to apply for any of the orders outlined above[56] and so would a father who had not been married to the mother at or at any time after the child's conception.[57]

7.33   Our provisional view is that other people should also be able to apply to the court for guardianship with care and control, although in some cases it would be desirable to require those first to obtain leave of the court.[58]   Applications could be made ex parte to avoid causing needless anxiety to parents or children in cases where there was no reasonable prospect of success.   This approach would mean that there was no need to make special provision for people who had treated the child as a member of their family or for the position after one or both parents had died.[59]

---

56   Including an order relating to a particular aspect of upbringing even if he no longer had guardianship or had only limited care and control.

57   This is the effect of the recommendation in Law Com. No. 118 (op. cit. at n. 36) that he should be able to apply to share specific "rights" with the mother.

58   See para. 5.39 above.

59   See Working Paper No. 91, paras. 3.48 to 3.50.

7.34   Where the child is in the care of a local authority, however, people with whom the child is boarded-out should only be able to apply (a) with the consent of the local authority or, if the child is in voluntary care, of each of his parents, or (b) where the child had his home with them for a certain length of time.   Currently this is three years and we invite views as to whether this might be reduced and if so to what period.[60]

7.35   The only non-parents who could apply for or be granted visiting orders, however, would be those who had treated the child as a member of their family, those who had previously been allocated parental responsibilities over him, and grandparents, uncles and aunts, or brothers and sisters (of the whole or half-blood, whether traced through marital or non-marital relationships).[61]

7.36   The only non-parents who could apply for particular questions to be resolved might be those who had already been allocated responsibility over that area.[62]   We invite views, however, as to whether those with a visiting order might also be given that right.   There are obvious risks that concerned grandparents might take too seriously the complaints of a child about particular matters (that risk already exists between parents on access visits) but they will also be better placed than most to know when something is seriously wrong.   However, the same would apply where they were able to visit without a court order.

The criteria for decision

7.37   In reaching any decision relating to the custody or upbringing of a child, the court should regard the welfare of the child as the

---

60   Paras. 5.41 to 5.48.

61   Para. 5.61-5.62.

62   As is the present law: see para. 2.50.

paramount consideration.[63]   It should also have to take into account the welfare of any other children "affected" [in the family][64] and (at least in contested cases) to ascertain the wishes and feelings of the child and give due consideration to them having regard to his age and understanding.[65]

7.38   In assessing the child's welfare, at least where guardianship or care and control is in issue, the court might be advised to have regard to the following factors along with all the circumstances of the case:[66]

> (1)   the quality of the love, affection and other emotional ties existing between the child and each of the parties;
>
> (2)   the nature of the emotional ties existing between the child and any person other than the parties;
>
> (3)   the effect upon the child of separation from either party or from any other person with whom he has been living;
>
> (4)   the capacity and disposition of each of the parties to provide for the child's emotional needs in the future, including the recognition of his ties with other people;
>
> (5)   the length of time the child has lived in his existing environment and the effect of any change, including changes of neighbourhood, school, local activities and access to relatives and friends;

---

63   Para. 6.22.

64   Para. 6.16.

65   Paras. 6.40-6.44.

66   Para. 6.38.

(6)   the capacity (bearing in mind any financial provision or property adjustment which may be ordered) and disposition of each of the parties to provide properly for the child's accommodation, hygiene, food, medical care appropriate supervision and companionship and otherwise for his physical needs and development;

(7)   the capacity (bearing in mind any financial provision which may be ordered) and disposition of each of the parties to provide properly for the child's education and intellectual development both at home and at school;

(8)   the capacity and disposition of each of the parties to provide properly for the child's social and ethical development;

(9)   where relevant the ethnic, cultural or religious background of the child and each of the parties;

(10)   the quality of the relationship existing or likely to exist between the child and any other member of each household and the likely effect of that member upon the capacities and dispositions of each of the parties in paragraphs (4), (6), (7) and (8) above;

(11)   any risk of ill-treatment by either party or by any present or likely member of that party's household;

(12)   any other special circumstances, including any particular aptitude or disability of the child;

(13)   the wishes and feelings of the child.

Private appointments

7.39 The scheme outlined in our paper on Guardianship for permitting parents to appoint a guardian privately[67] could readily be incorporated in the above structure. Thus a parent would be able by deed or will to appoint a guardian:

(i) to replace him after his death;

(ii) to replace him temporarily during a period of illness or absence abroad; or

(iii) to share his responsibilities where he was sole guardian of the child.

7.40 Such a guardian would share the same responsibilities as one appointed by the court. Neither would have power to appoint a guardian,[68] save that an unmarried father who had been granted guardianship would retain his present power to do so.

Other matters

7.41 Our main purpose in this paper has been to discuss the general shape of the substantive law. We have not dealt with all the issues raised by the analysis of the existing law in Part II. Some of these will fall by the wayside if our preferred approach is adopted. Others cannot be properly considered until the broad outlines of the substantive law are

---

67 Working Paper No. 91, paras. 4.4 to 4.31.

68 Ibid., para. 3.74 invites views on this issue.

known or initiatives elsewhere which could affect them are more advanced.[69]

7.42   A number of such issues have been raised by the Review of Child Care Law or are connected with its proposals. These are:

(1)   representation of the child, not only when committal to local authority care is contemplated but also in other cases;[70]

(2)   the procedural implications of assimilating the grounds and effects of committal to care in family proceedings with those of care orders made in care proceedings;[71]

(3)   the powers of the court to make interim orders, where committal to care is contemplated or in other cases;[72]

(4)   the grounds for and effects of supervision orders made in family proceedings;[73]

---

69   E.g. research currently being carried out on behalf of D.H.S.S. by the Socio-Legal Centre for Family Studies at Bristol University into the representation of children in civil proceedings and the Consultation Paper published by the Interdepartmental Review of Family and Domestic Jurisdiction, May 1986.

70   See para. 2.80 to 2.86 and 6.40 to 6.44; Review of Child Care Law ("R.C.C.L.") (1985), para. 14.18, recommended that the Commission should consider representation where committal to care is contemplated.

71   See para. 2.68 and R.C.C.L., para. 16.41.

72   For interim custody orders, see paras. 2.70 and 2.71; there is at present no power to make an interim care order and the matter is not covered by R.C.C.L.

73   See paras. 2.60 to 2.64 and R.C.C.L., paras. 18.26 to 18.29.

(5)   the proposed power of a court in care proceedings to make custody and related orders.[74]

We plan to return to these issues later in our review and to discuss them in the light of, among other things, the Government's White Paper in response to the Review of Child Care Law.[75]

C.   The form of the new scheme

7.43   The final aspect of the possible new system which we have yet to discuss is whether or not it should take the form of a single code.[76] This is far from a purely technical or presentational matter and requires consideration against the overall objectives of the law in this area.   By a "code", in this context, we do not mean a definitive or immutable statement of all the law relating to children but a set of coherent and comprehensive statutory provisions which should remain consistent despite amendments.   The main arguments for and against a code are as follows:-

The advantages of a code

7.44 (1)   The allocation of parental responsibilities, and the courts' powers to deal with those responsibilities in private law, would be brought together in a single statute.   All inconsistencies of policy and terminology would be removed.   Where it was necessary to draw distinctions, for example between parental and third party claims, these could be more clearly structured and expressed.

---

74   See paras. 2.7 and 2.79 and R.C.C.L., paras. 19.7 to 19.9, 19.11 and 20.27.

75   See Hansard (H.C.) vol. 96, Written Answers, cols. 472 and 473.

76   See para. 1.2 above.

(2)   Inconsistencies arising because of amendments to one statute but not to others should no longer arise.

(3)   The reallocation of parental responsibility would be seen to be a single jurisdiction, rather than several. There would be no duplication of provisions and the complicated incorporation of provisions by reference would be eliminated. Matters such as the effect of over-lapping orders[77] could readily be clarified.

(4)   Such an exercise would itself constitute an incentive towards greater simplicity.

(5)   The consolidation of the Guardianship of Minors Act 1971, Guardianship Act 1973 and relevant parts of the Children Act 1975 is in any event desirable; the number and complexity of enactments will be increased if the Child Custody Bill[78] and Family Law Reform Bill[79] become law.

(6)   The severance of questions of parental responsibility from other issues between the adults should emphasise that the future of children is important in its own right and not simply as an ancillary matter in matrimonial and other disputes.

---

77   See paras. 2.77 to 2.79.

78   Annexed to Custody of Children - Jurisdiction and Enforcement within the United Kingdom (1985) Law Com. No. 138, Scot. Law Com. No. 91, now Part I of the Family Law Bill 1986.

79   Annexed to Law Com. No. 118 (op. cit. at n. 36).

(7)   The existence of a matrimonial dispute between spouses should not, of itself, provide a greater occasion for interfering in parental responsibilities than would otherwise exist. A single code would provide the opportunity to rationalise the occasions upon which a duty to give special consideration to the children's future should arise.

The disadvantages of a code

7.45 (1)   It is certain to remain the case that the question of custody will often arise in the course of matrimonial proceedings; despite its great importance, custody is only part of the family's problems; isolating it from that context may serve to confuse rather than to clarify matters.

(2)   In particular, if the courts are to retain their responsibility to consider the arrangements made for the children when a marriage breaks up, confusion will be caused if such duties are separated from the matrimonial jurisdictions in which they arise, or, on the other hand, from the powers to make orders in consequence.

(3)   The provisions relating to financial support and property adjustment in favour of children would cause particular difficulty. Financial provision for children is part of their welfare, and if not brought within the single statute, the statute would be incomplete. Yet the severance of provision for the children from provision for the adults would be equally artificial and could cause difficulties in practice. It is now the law that, in determining provision for both the adults and the children involved, the court must give first consideration to the welfare of the children.

Conclusion

7.46   There appear to us, therefore, to be three main options:

232

(i)   to collect into a single statute the provisions of the Guardianship Act 1973, the Guardianship of Minors Act 1971, and the portions of the Children Act 1975 dealing with custodianship and the explanation of concepts, and to amend the Matrimonial Causes Act 1973 and Domestic Proceedings and Magistrates' Courts Act 1978 to achieve such consistency as is possible;

(ii)   to collect all the provisions dealing with custody, access and related matters, but to set out the court's duty to consider the arrangements for children involved in divorce and other matrimonial proceedings, and perhaps the provisions dealing with financial relief and property adjustment for them in the statutes relating to those proceedings; and

(iii)   to collect all the provisions relating to children into a single, comprehensive and consistent code.

7.47   To some extent, the choice between these courses depends upon the nature of the reform which is eventually adopted. If the system outlined above were to find favour, the case for option (iii) would be enhanced; if, on the other hand, for example, it were thought that the powers of divorce courts should remain radically different from those in the other jurisdictions, the case for a single statute would be diminished. Our provision preference, therefore, lies between (ii) and (iii).

Printed in the UK for HMSO
Dd 739296 C15 7/86